Barns

A Sampling of Iowa's Round Barns

© *Photo by Carolyn Fox*

*Cameron Round Barn Roof Interior,
Taylor County Museum Grounds,
Bedford, Iowa*

Photographs by Luella Hazeltine

Edited by Deb Schense

Dedicated to the preservers of round barns in Iowa.

Acknowledgments: Mary Bennett and Lowell Soike of the State Historical Society of Iowa. Thanks to all barn owners who allowed us to photograph their barns, or who supplied photographs. Permission was granted by the owners for these photographs to be published.

Front Cover: Hendecagonal Barn, Kossuth County, Buffalo Township, Section 2, Eleven-Sided Barn, built in 1910. This barn burned May 29, 2003.

Back Cover:
Top: Henry County, Jackson Township, Section 32, Holtkamp True-Round Barn built in 1918.

Center: Johnson County, Schwab True-Round Barn built in 1992.

Below: Allamakee County, Thomas Reburn Twelve-Sided Barn built in 1914.

Associate Editors: Dwayne and Joan Liffring-Zug Bourret, Melinda Bradnan, Miriam Canter, Dorothy Crum, Jacque Gharib, David Heusinkveld, Jeff Schense, Connie Schnoebelen, David and Jeanne Wright.
Graphic Design: Rodger Rufer and M. A. Cook Design, Molly Cook
Technical Assistance: David Trawick

— **Barn Books by Mail** —
Barns Around Iowa: A Sampling of Iowa's Round Barns
Penfield Books, 215 Brown Street, Iowa City, Iowa 52245-5801.
$18.95 postpaid. Iowans add 6% sales tax. Prices subject to change.
1-800-728-9998   Fax: 319-351-6846
Penfield Books website: http://www.penfieldbooks.com
Penfield e-mail: penfield@penfieldbooks.com
Complete catalog of all titles $2.50.
Books are available for fundraisers. Please call Penfield for information.

Eastern Iowa's Historic Barns and Other Farm Structures: Including the Amana Colonies by Deb Schense preserves in print Eastern Iowa's historic barns built from 1839 to 1955 in an 8-1/2x11" format.
Black and white edition $19.89 ($24.69 postpaid) with 250 photographs.
Color edition $39.89 ($44.69 postpaid) with 175 photographs.
Prices subject to change. Retail only. You may order these books at:
Penfield Books, 215 Brown Street, Iowa City, Iowa 52245-5801 or order online at: http://stores.lulu.com/dschense   Deb's e-mail: dschense@netins.net

ISBN-13: 978-193204344-0
ISBN-10: 193204344-6
Library of Congress 2008925518

©2008 Penfield Books

Contents

Luella's Search for
  Round Barns 6-10
History of the Round Barn 11
  A Replica of George Washington's
    Sixteen-sided Barn 12
Discovery and
  Preservation 13-14
  Discovering Round Barns in
    North America 13-14
Types of Round Barns 15
  Octagon Barns and
    Multi-sided Barns 15
  Round Barns 15
  True-round Barns 15-16
A Lost Barn 16
Hen House in
  Allamakee County 17
Adair County
  Greenfield 18
  Orient 19
Allamakee County
  Dorchester 20
  Luana 21
  New Albin 22
  Postville 23
  Waukon 24
Audubon County
  Audubon 25
Benton County
  La Porte City 26-27
Black Hawk County
  Cedar Falls 28-30
  Dunkerton 31

Bremer County
  Plainfield 32
  Waverly 33
Buchanan County
  Hazleton 34
  Jesup 35
Buena Vista County
  Alta 35
  Storm Lake 36
Calhoun County
  Manson 37-39
Carroll County
  Manning 40
Cedar County
  Tipton 41
Cerro Gordo County
  Mason City 41-42
Chickasaw County
  Charles City 43
Clayton County
  Guttenberg 44-45
Dallas County
  Bouton 46
Decatur County
  Leon 47
Delaware County
  Coggon 48
Dickinson County
  Milford 49
Dubuque County
  Dubuque 50

Emmet County
  Armstrong 51
Fayette County
  Arlington 52
  Randalia 53
  West Union 54-55
Floyd County
  Charles City 56
Franklin County
  Iowa Falls 57
Hamilton County
  Blairsburg 58
Hancock County
  Forest City 59
Hardin County
  Iowa Falls 60
Harrison County
  Moorhead 61
Henry County
  Salem 62
Howard County
  Cresco 63
Ida County
  Cushing 64
Iowa County
  Marengo 65
Jackson County
  Bellevue 66
Jasper County
  Monroe 67-68
Johnson County
  Riverside 68
  Iowa City 69
  Solon 70-73

Johnson County (continued)
  West Liberty 74-76
Keokuk County
  Webster 77
Kossuth County
  Algona 78-79
  Titonka 80
Lee County
  Fort Madison 81
Linn County
  Alburnett 82
Lyon County
  Rock Rapids 83
Madison County
  Winterset 84-85
Mahaska County
  Oskaloosa 85-86
Marion County
  Knoxville 87
Marshall County
  Marshalltown 88
  Melbourne 89
  State Center 90
  History of the Round Barn
     Mail-order Kits 91-93
Monona County
  Mapleton 94
Montgomery County
  Red Oak 95
  Villisca 96
Page County
  Clarinda 97
  Essex 97
  Shenandoah 98

Plymouth County
  Akron 99
  Le Mars 100

Pocahontas County
  Pocahontas 101

Pottawattamie County
  Silver City 102

Poweshiek County
  Montezuma 103

Ringgold County
  Diagonal 104

Scott County
  Davenport 105-106
  Le Claire 107

Sioux County
  Garfield 108

Story County
  Nevada 109
  Ames 109

Tama County
  Dysart 110
  Traer 111

Taylor County
  Bedford 112-113
  Blockton 113

Van Buren County
  Cantril 114-115
  Douds 115
  Farmington 116

Warren County
  Milo 117

Washington County
  Riverside 118
  Wellman 119

Wayne County
  Allerton 120

Winnebago County
  Scarville 121

Winneshiek County
  Burr Oak 122
  Decorah 123-124

About the Photographer
  Luella Hazeltine 125

About the Editor
  Deb M. Schense 125

Giants of Agriculture 126

Bakkum Pines 127

Map of Iowa Barn Sites 128

The word cupola comes from Latin, meaning "little cupo" or "little dome." Roof cupolas save money by allowing the moisture and hot air inside the building to escape. This helps prevent wood rot, mildew, and paint peeling.

The cupola is traced back to eighth-century Islamic architecture. It is a design to allow venting and airing out of mosques while keeping the weather out.

Photo by Deb Schense

Luella's Search for Round Barns

Photo by Joan Liffring-Zug Bourret

Luella Hazeltine of Toddville, Iowa, and Dick Schwab of rural Solon stand in front of his true-round barn made of Stone City, Iowa, stone.

My name is Luella Hazeltine. My first experience with round barns was on my honeymoon in August 1953. We had a flat tire and the spare was also flat, but it was my fault since it was my car. While we waited for help to arrive, we got out a blanket and sat in the shade of an apple tree. At the bottom of the hill, was the Ten Eyk Apple Orchard near Monroe, Wisconsin. They had a beautiful round barn. Since then, we have passed that barn many times, and I took many photographs of it, thinking it was unique.

In the fall of 1993, I taped a public television program about the "Round Barns of Iowa." One of the barns on the show was the Secrest Octagonal barn in Johnson County. I was fascinated and wanted to find out where it was located.

My niece Linda Heath drove a delivery truck in the area. She knew where three barns were located. I asked her to show me. At the first place we went in Lincoln Township, we were told the owner of the barn had burned it a few weeks earlier.

Our second stop was the Miller barn. We couldn't find the third barn that day.

However, I did find the Roberts Octagonal barn after making a wrong turn.

I took my sister Billie and her granddaughter d'Lyse to see the barns. Later, d'Lyse wanted to take Grandma Arlene to see the barns. After a few days, we took my sister Arlene and d'Lyse's sister Rachael to see them too.

After seeing the barns in our area, Arlene asked, "Are there any other barns in the area we can go see?" I went to the Cedar Rapids library and checked out a book on round barns, *Without Right Angles: The Round Barns of Iowa* by Lowell Soike, published by the State Historical Society of Iowa. After reading it, I bought a copy. It had a list of round barns. I found one in Poweshiek County so we planned our next trip there. When we arrived, the owner shared some of the history associated with the barn.

After visiting all of the round barns listed for Eastern Iowa, we mapped a course for the barns farther away and started to make overnight trips. We were hooked. We didn't want to stop. At some point, we decided we had to see all the round barns in Iowa, and that's exactly what we did.

We took Rachael Strickel and d'Lyse Abukaf on most of our barn trips until they moved to Florida. At times other family members came along such as my brother Ralph Heath, my sister Bessie Beaty, my sister-in-law Jinny Heath, my best friend Verlea Staats, and anyone else I could find. There were plenty of volunteers. Although my husband was not interested in the search, he enjoyed seeing the pictures.

Arlene was always the navigator. We even told the girls which direction to look. They both wanted to be the first one to spot the barn. They were our "chief barn spotters." We taught them to read maps, plot the course to the next barn, and how to follow highway signs. The girls became familiar with many road signs, especially speed limit, overpass, underpass, and detour signs.

Our only directions were county and township names along with section numbers. Although I had maps, they were from the 1950s. This made it hard to follow the new road construction. The girls would say, "Let's go ask a man." So, we asked a lot of men and occasionally we asked a woman. The kids learned a lot about farms and barns. The farmers were always glad to educate the "city kids." I was glad the girls were learning about farming. One thing we learned is that wind always blows around a round barn, and there is no place to escape the wind.

We also learned jokes related to the "no corners" in a round barn. One joke was that a cat went crazy because it couldn't find a corner in which to relieve itself. Another joke was the farmer was late for supper because he couldn't find a corner to place his pitchfork.

Our kids loved the dogs and cats on the farms. When we opened the car door and a dog crawled in, the kids were delighted. They laughed when a dog would walk around the exterior of the car, urinating on all four tires.

Most barn owners enjoyed their barns and were proud to talk about them. Occasionally we met a few who did not like their barns and wanted to tear down the "old things." One group bought an unwanted barn and moved it to a summer campsite approximately a mile away.

In Monona County we couldn't find anyone who had ever seen a round barn in the area. I finally gave up and turned around in a driveway. Later, I wrote to the courthouse and asked for information. They sent a map with the barn location. Although the barn was on the property where I had been, there was no way to see it from the road without driving up the hill and into the yard. Many barns can only be seen from one direction, so we backtracked and asked residents and even flagged down passing motorists.

It surprises me how many people don't pay any attention to their neighborhood surroundings. People would say, "I've never seen a round barn, and I've lived here 50 years," yet, just around the corner there would be a large round barn in plain sight. One person insisted there was no such thing in the entire county. When we finally located the barn, it was only three-fourths of a mile away, in plain sight from his house, and there were two others in the same county.

When scouting for barns, I would always talk to the owners before walking around their property. This is how I got so many stories and histories of the barns. Courtesy is always the best policy. An amusing thing that happened on one of our trips was when three-year-old d'Lyse asked a farmer, "Is this your barn?"

He replied, "Yes it is, right out there."

"Is it on the National Register?" she asked.

Surprised that a three-year-old knew of the National Register of Historic Places, he replied, "Yes it is."

At another farm, a kid on a bike between my camera and the barn, asked what we were doing. I explained that I only wanted a picture of the round barn. He said, "I'm going to be famous." I explained the picture was only for me, but he kept saying, "I'm going to be famous." The boy and his bike appear in all the pictures that I took of the barn. At the time the barn was being restored. The boy has since moved away.

In Franklin County there was a low-flat-roofed round barn. The owner told us he kept a pail of tar on the roof, and he would put a fresh coat on a section, going around section-by-section as time allowed.

In Floyd County I drove up and down the roads looking for a round barn. Finally, I went into a farmyard where I saw some people. I asked, "Do you know where there is a round barn?"

The lady answered, "It was right over there, but you are a year too late." She pointed to a pile of boards and said, "A windstorm ruined it so we pulled it down for safety reasons. One of our friends asked for the lumber to build a garage. We told him he could have it. When he is finished taking all of the boards he wants, we will burn the rest."

In Delaware County the owner was training a team of horses to pull a wagon. He said his great-grandfather, at a cost of $1,900, built the barn. His great-grandfather had already laid the foundation for a regular barn, but then he saw a round barn in Missouri. When he came home, he tore out the foundation and built a round clay tile barn. The barn has been repaired and is still in use.

In Page County we saw a sixteen-sided barn high on a hill. We couldn't get very close because the gate was locked. Fortunately, I had a telephoto lens. Between the barn and the road was a forest of walnut trees. As Billie looked at the trees, she recalled that in 1967, her son Tim had worked on a tree planting crew in Page County. When we got home, she asked her son just where they had planted trees in the county. He told her and then said, "Oh, there was a sixteen-sided barn on the hill." That's exactly where we had been.

Wherever we stopped to eat, we chatted with the locals, asking if they knew where any round barns were. Sometimes they knew and sometimes they didn't. Arlene kept track of the directions to them. It got easier when the emergency 911 numbers were put in use. Iowa didn't get the 911 address numbers completed at the same time, but we did our best.

In Cedar Falls our waitress noticed we were looking at a map and asked if she could help. We said we were looking for round barns. She said, "Do you have the one just off 218 in Bremer County?" She gave us directions, and we drove right to it. It was being used as an antique shop. The house was built from the same type of clay tile, and their mailbox was a miniature hexagon barn.

In Taylor County we went to a listed barn location and learned that a crew had carefully taken the barn apart and reassembled it in the Historical Park in Bedford. When we got there, it had been restored and painted light yellow. The man had hired a crew of Amish craftsmen to do the work. They are about the only ones who will do this difficult work. For example, three-tab roofing requires a lot of cutting to fit on the round cone roof. Others also had hired the Amish workers to do repairs.

It was always nice to find a descendant of the original owner of the farm. He or she was always proud of the barn and often said, "We built it and we still own it." There are many barns still in the family of the original builder. The last name may be different, but this only means it descended from the female family lineage.

We talked with a second-generation owner who told us how his father and uncle had worked on the project. The foundation trench was dug six feet deep and two feet wide. The men dug the trench by hand. A few years ago, the cupola was damaged in a storm, and they could not find a place to buy a new one. They hired Mennonites to rebuild it and install it on the roof. The owner was glad to have found someone else to repair it because he had climbed to the top once, and the wind almost blew him off the roof.

In Wright County we talked to the owner of a barn who told us his story. A windstorm had damaged the roof beyond repair. A roofless barn isn't a useful building, so he had decided to tear it down. It was a much harder job than anticipated because clay tile barns are made with two layers of tile and six inches of air space in between. The owner said, "If I had known how hard it would be to tear it down, it would still be standing, and the neighbors would be happy to have their landmark for giving directions."

We were always glad to see barns being repaired. In Story County I drove past a barn just to make sure I had the right address. The owner was up on the roof repairing the damage from a lightning bolt. I drove in to tell him how happy I was to see him repairing his barn.

In Webster County we spotted an intriguing building and drove toward it. There was a cluster of houses and a round grain elevator. I waved down a pickup truck and asked, "Did this used to be a town?"

He replied, "It still is." Oops. The town's name is Tara.

Later, we heard about a round barn in Polk County that was moved and restored. After it was moved, someone burned it down. They discovered it had been arson. That happened just a few weeks before we were there.

I always carried the barn photo album in the car. Almost every farmer we visited was interested in seeing the photos, even those who didn't own a round barn.

We believe we have seen every existing round barn in Iowa and have found many that are not in Lowell Soike's book, *Without Right Angles: The Round Barns of Iowa*. We used the 911 addresses for the places that had completed the service in their area.

Although I tried to be accurate, I probably have made a few mistakes. I took most of the pictures and for those I didn't take, I've included the name of the photographer listed below each picture.

Most barns are on gravel roads, so expect to get your car a little dusty. We enjoyed the years of adventure, and are now photographing barns in Illinois and Wisconsin.

Looking back, I'm glad that I saw the television show on round barns, that Arlene had asked about "more barns," and that I went to the Cedar Rapids public library to research round barns. If these things hadn't happened, I never would have started this wonderful journey photographing the barns pictured in this book. I would have missed out on a great time with my family, and my nieces would not have learned so much about farming and round barns.

—Luella Hazeltine, photographer*
All photographs are by Luella Hazeltine, unless indicated otherwise.

Five different glaciers formed the Iowa plains. The last glacier, which blanketed about one-fifth of the state, retreated from the north central region approximately 10,000 years ago, leaving behind the richest black topsoil in the United States. This soil was especially well-suited for agriculture.

History of the Round Barn

One of the nation's first round barns was a sixteen-sided structure designed and built in 1792 by George Washington. Washington wanted an indoor place to thresh grain at his Dogue Run Farm in Fairfax County, Virginia. Horses were led up an earthen ramp to the second floor and were led around the perimeter to tread out and separate the grain from the chaff. In the fall of 1992, exactly two hundred years after the original barn was designed, staff members at George Washington's estate developed plans to build a replica of his barn. Using period methods of construction, the building began in the spring of 1995. Construction was finished in fall 1996. (See page 12 for a picture of the replica of George Washington's barn.)

The Shakers at Hancock, Massachusetts, built the next historic round barn of note in 1826. Nearly a half-century passed before American farmers built additional octagonal barns.

Ahead of his time, in 1867, Lorenzo S. Coffin had a livestock farm near Fort Dodge, Iowa, and was the first Iowan to build an eight-sided barn. Coffin built his barn with two entrances: one featured a lower level built into a hillside and a second upper level for easy entry by horses pulling loads. Coffin, a farm editor for the *Fort Dodge Messenger,* and Benjamin F. Gue, editor of the *Iowa Homestead,* promoted the octagonal barn. Farmers debated the virtues of octagonal versus rectangular barns. After 90 years of service, Coffin's barn collapsed in the 1960s.

Elliott W. Stewart, farmer, lecturer at Cornell University and editor of a farm publication, built an octagonal barn with clear loft space, made possible by a superior roof design using an octagonal cone. He built this prototype barn near Buffalo, New York, to replace four rectangular barns that burned in 1874. Stewart and farm journalists promoted and published octagonal barn plans.

Although some Iowans built smaller versions in the 1870s, by the 1880s and 1890s, more Iowans were building large eight-sided barns with varying roof designs. Typically, concrete foundations replaced limestone after 1889. As a result of the promotions by agricultural colleges and experimental stations, Midwestern farmers built the majority of round barns in America. Fulton County, Indiana, and the state of Wisconsin claim to have the most round barns. An annual Round Barn Festival is held in Fulton County. Round barn sites and information are available on the Internet for structures in over forty states.

Nomadic Paleo-Indian tribes lived in Iowa 12,000 years ago. Large game hunting drew them to the area. Nomadic hunters of the archaic period occupied the land around 8,500 years ago, followed by the Woodland Indians. In more recent times, the Ioway Indians gave their name to the state. Historical evidence shows that they grew corn, beans, pumpkins, and squash.

Courtesy of the Mount Vernon Ladies' Association

A Replica of George Washington's Sixteen-sided Barn

The original 52-foot diameter barn took George Washington's carpenters two years to complete. This replica was completed in 1996, using old photographs as a guide, almost two hundred years after the original barn was built. The original foundation was constructed using 30,820 bricks, while the upper floor was made of wooden planks. An interior lane circled the center for threshing. Horses were encouraged to run around the heart of the barn to separate the wheat grain from the chaff. If the horses were kept running, they would not urinate or defecate. The grain fell through the gaps in the floorboards to the lower level where it was gathered for grinding into flour.

George Washington's Mount Vernon Estate and Gardens is located 16 miles south of Washington D. C., and is open year round to the public. George Washington was the first president of the United States from 1789–1797.

The first meeting between white men and Illinois Indians took place on June 25, 1673, on Iowa soil with the arrival of a French explorer, Louis Joliet, Father Jacques Marquette, and a five member French expedition team.

Discovery and Preservation

In a statewide survey conducted in the 1970s, the Iowa Historic Preservation Office discovered 160 structures, instead of the forty round barns they expected to find. Round barns are located in all but eighteen of the state's ninety-nine counties. Over a decade of research and photography by historians and photographers followed. Their efforts resulted in the 1983 publication of the book, *Without Right Angles: The Round Barns of Iowa,* by Lowell J. Soike of the State Historical Society of Iowa's Office of Historic Preservation.

Soike's landmark work was the guide to Luella Hazeltine's ten-plus years project of documenting, in color, many of these barns. Her original photographic work is preserved in the growing collection of barn photography at the State Historical Society of Iowa.

Unless a concerted effort is made to preserve them, all nineteenth and twentieth-century wood barns in Iowa, whether round or rectangular, are threatened. Of the 60,000 barns in Iowa, an estimated one thousand barns of all shapes are lost annually. Founded in 1997, the non-profit Iowa Barn Foundation works to increase public awareness of these cultural landmarks and provides barn restoration matching grants. Private property owners, who, at their own expense, rehabilitate their barns receive Awards of Distinction. *The Iowa Barn Foundation* magazine is available by subscription. The foundation annually sponsors regional tours as well as an All-State Barn Tour.

Note: It is estimated that 1,000 Iowa barns disappear every year. This book preserves in print Iowa's heritage of approximately 100 of Iowa's agricultural barns. Some of the barns in this book are no longer standing.

For more information on restoration grants or tours, please visit: http://www.iowabarnfoundation.org

DISCOVERING ROUND BARNS IN NORTH AMERICA

You will find scores of colorful photographs and stories of round barns located in the United States and Canada on the Internet. The largest concentration of round barns, is found in the Midwest. Midwestern cities even play host to annual round barn festivals, where activities are planned to entertain the entire family, with proceeds promoting the restoration efforts of all kinds of barns.

Because many of the round barns in the Midwest are at the century mark, they need essential repairs such as new roofs, shingles, siding, painting, or foundation work. Several community groups have formed to assist in preserving these historical landmarks for future generations. Repair costs rise well into the thousands of dollars. The world wide web plays a key role in restoration efforts by posting the names of barn restoration businesses and financial assistance programs to facilitate much-needed barn repairs. Some web sites also list used barn wood to be sold or given away to help barn owners make repairs with similarly aged wood.

The Internet enables families to pass on their barn stories and for others to share their efforts in transforming their round barns into lodges, restaurants, inns, bed-and-breakfasts, or houses.

Because annual historical barn tours are so popular, there are not enough seats on the buses to meet demand. Many people follow tour buses with their own transportation.

Perhaps you want to create and share your own adventure on the web, in a blog, or on the pages of a book, as Luella Hazeltine has shared with us. Put a little gas in the car or fire up the computer; jump on the back roads or cruise the Internet highway to create your own round-barn adventure.

—Deb Schense, Editor

Barn Identification
We have identified barns by the last name of the persons who built them. In some cases, successive owners have asked that their names be added to the builder's name of the barn.

Barn Courtesy
We suggest that you, please, knock at the front door of each property's dwelling and communicate your intentions before walking around the barn owner's private property. This way the residents will know why you are on their property. Thank you.

Barn Information
Information about the barns featured in this book is omitted following the photograph only when there is no history available.

The French ruled the Midwest until 1763 when it was given to the King of Spain. In 1801, a treaty was signed granting the land back to the French. In 1803, President Jefferson purchased the land from Napoleon for $15 million. This was known as the Louisiana Purchase, which included Iowa.

Types of Round Barns

Octagon Barns and Multi-sided Barns

Eight-sided octagon barns were popular among farmers. Many used ingenuity in building their own variations. The sixteen-sided barn with a self-supporting roof was popular from the 1880s to the 1890s. This structure often contains a loft with unobstructed space. Iowans also built twelve-sided, ten-sided, and six-sided ones. Other versions included an eleven-sided barn, one with thirteen sides, and nine-sided barns. In addition to barns, some farmers built hog houses in a circular pattern, making it easier to feed livestock.

Round Barns with a Circular Silo and Clay tile

Modern barn designs became popular after 1900. Franklin H. King, professor of physics at the Wisconsin Agricultural Experiment Station in Madison, designed the Wisconsin (or King) all-wood silo, centered in the barn structure. The Illinois Experiment Station in Champaign made improvements in natural light enhancement. These Champaign designers confirmed the desirability of the self-supporting roof as a basic feature of the round barn, eliminating obstructions and support beams in the hayloft storage area.

Additional experiments in silo construction at the Iowa Experiment Station in Ames led to use of hollow and curved clay tile, creating a building known as the Iowa barn type, sixty feet in diameter with a 16- by 46-foot silo at its center. Two stories high, this barn held a 10- by 15-foot water tank at its top. Original plans called for a concrete floor (a new product at this time), with clay block walls and a self-supporting roof. Its interior contained space for 36 stalls facing inward. Two entrances led to a second floor with a dairy room below. As a result of work conducted at the Experiment Station, more efficiently designed round barns were built in the Midwest in the years preceding and during World War I.

The majority of clay tile enhanced barns were located north of Interstate 80 that divides the Midwest, because there were more dairy farmers in Northeast Iowa than anywhere in the state. Round, wood barns, less expensive to build, appeared in Southern Iowa. Barns of timber were constructed all over Iowa but were especially popular in Eastern Iowa, where wood was plentiful.

True-round Barns

After 1890, true-round barns appeared in Iowa. They featured interiors similar to those of the rectangular structures, as well as mangers, feeding and cleaning areas, and box stalls in a circle, usually arranged around a silo. The roof was self-supporting. Clay tile was often preferred over all-wood building materials, especially for sanitary reasons. Samples of true-round barns follow.

A Lost Barn

Photo by Joan Liffring-Zug Bourret

ALLAMAKEE COUNTY, POST TOWNSHIP, SECTION 2

This true-round barn was still standing in the late 1980s, but no longer exists today. This photograph graced the back cover of the 1990 second printing of the book by Lowell Soike, Without Right Angles: The Round Barns of Iowa.

The Great Depression of the late 1920s and early 1930s brought an end to the construction of round barns in Iowa. The increasing use of engine-driven equipment, the size of equipment, and the decline of the horse as a main component in farming were contributing factors. Today, round barns are preserved or re-created only by the few who cherish this historic and beautiful building type.

Hen House in Allamakee County

Engraving by John Page

Printmaker John Page, University of Northern Iowa Professor Emeritus, made this engraving of the round hen house above.

Photo by Joan Liffring-Zug Bourret

This hen house photograph shows the architecture of a true-round barn.

Adair County

612 SW 2ND STREET, GREENFIELD

This barn is no longer standing.

Iowa was officially opened to settlement on June 1, 1833. Before dawn, the settlers made a mad dash for the land. They even floated their wagons across the Mississippi River. Squatter's rights were in effect until the surveyors finished surveying the land. Land sales began in 1838 for $1.25 an acre. The threshing machine was patented in 1837.

— Adair County —

Octagonal Hog Barn, L & E Acres Inc., Union Township, Section 16, Orient

This eight-sided hog barn with balloon frame construction has horizontal drop siding. A large inner cupola with an octagonal roof sits on an eight-piece, wood-shingled roof. Windows give additional light on the far side.

The history of the State of Iowa has been called "inseparably intertwined with its agricultural productivity." This fertile quadrangle, was settled in the year 1788 and became a state in 1846. Iowa contains 56,290 square miles and ranks 25th in land area. Iowa and its citizens have led the nation and the world in the development and production of agricultural prosperity.

Allamakee County

DODECAGONAL BARN, 2856 HIGHWAY 76, DORCHESTER

Built by Henry Weber in 1911, this twelve-sided basement barn is ramped to the loft and has a two-pitched gambrel roof. On top of the roof is a cupola with an octagonal cone-type roof. Since this picture was taken, the barn has been painted red with white trim and the aluminum was replaced on the roof.

Some people believed that the round barn came about because of the circular construction of Indian teepees. Others believed the roundhouses used to rotate the steam locomotives may have influenced the invention of the round barn.

— Allamakee County —

Lamborn Barn, 224 Franklin Road, Luana

The owner's great-grandfather, Elba Lamborn, built this round barn on the family farm in 1911. Framed with home-sawn oak sitting on a concrete foundation, the barn has an entry-level dairy cattle area, a loft level above, and a central hay chute in the center. The ground level area has a spherical arrangement with a manger, cow stanchions, and a gutter adjoining a central hay chute. In the late 1950s, asphalt shingles were placed over the cedar shingles and in the early 1960s a milk-house was added to the east side. In 2003, this barn was torn down because of a poor foundation.

The English used to put a roof over the horses for shelter while they walked in a circle to power mills. This may have been a predecessor to the round barn.

— Allamakee County —

Thomas Reburn Dodecagonal Barn, 1641 Pool Hill Drive, New Albin

Built by Thomas Reburn in 1914, this twelve-sided 46-foot diameter barn includes a 14-foot diameter silo one story higher than the roof. The circular feeding area around the silo feeds 50 cattle simultaneously. The silo roof, which had the same pitch as the barn, was replaced after a windstorm in the mid-1950s. A concrete block foundation was used for the barn and silo. Located just southwest of New Albin, this barn is on the National Register of Historic Places. The silo is still used and cattle are fed around its base.

Iowa State University was established in 1858 as the Iowa Agricultural College. Iowans have always placed high priority on education, and the establishment of this college in Ames captured their conviction that higher education should be accessible to all and that such a college should teach practical subjects. These ideals were integral to the thinking that led to land-grant universities.

— Allamakee County —

812 Jackson Hollow Drive, Postville

A.W. Swenson hired Otto Sanders in 1914 to construct this wood-frame barn of native logs sawed into dimension plank lumber. Its foundation (ten feet high and two feet thick) is made with stone quarried from the farm. The barn measures 50 feet in diameter, and a hay manger wraps around its interior wall. The manger is fed via hay chutes along the outside perimeter of the loft story. A self-supporting gambrel roof covers all. Unfortunately, this landmark building collapsed on a clear calm day in September, 2002.

After Lincoln signed The Federal Land Grant College Act in 1862, Iowa was the first state to accept the provisions of the new legislation for its college in Ames. The first students arrived in Ames in 1869 and graduated in 1872. The school's progressive and inventive spirit made it a leader, then and now, in the fields of agriculture, engineering, extension services, veterinary medicine, and computer sciences.

— Allamakee County —

Meyer Barn, 1158 North Fork Hollow Road, Waukon

This 1912 barn construction is referred to as the bank barn design, with a lower story constructed of stone, and the upper, wood-framed loft accessed by a ramp embankment built into its north face. It possesses two features that make it unique. Both its siding and its interior silo are rare finds in Iowa. The exterior siding is constructed of horizontally sawn wood while the silo is constructed of a wood stave lined with cement inside. Such silos were popular until the 1910s, but are exceedingly rare today. Sadly, in July 2002, this structure was lost to a storm.

Republicans ruled state politics in the 1850s, quickly instigating changes. They moved the state capital from Iowa City to Des Moines, created the University of Iowa, and drafted a new state constitution. The Republican Party opposed slavery and promoted land ownership, banking, and railroads.

Audubon County

Photo by Rachael Strickel

2083 Robin Avenue, Audubon

Thomas Campbell built this true-round Campbell barn in 1916. It is a general-purpose barn constructed of hollow-clay tile from Adel, Iowa, and stands 60 feet in diameter reaching 18 feet at its eaves. The two-pitched gambrel-designed roof with a hay dormer and gabled roof overhang was replaced after severe windstorm damage in 1959.

The Iowa State Fair didn't always have its roots in Des Moines, Iowa. The first and second fairs were held in Fairfield, Iowa, in 1854 and 1855.

Benton County

1088 52nd Street, La Porte City

The J. G. McQuilkin round barn was built in 1914. Another of the sixteen hollow-clay tile round barns built by the Johnston Brothers Clay Works, this 60-foot barn, once used for housing horses, has since been converted to raising pigs and cattle. In the heart of the barn stands a 14-foot diameter silo with a cone-shaped roof. A gabled hay dormer extends from the roof, which is covered with asphalt shingles.

A round barn from 60 to 90 feet in diameter can hold approximately one hundred dairy cows with room to spare.

— Benton County —

5075 11th Avenue, La Porte City

This 1914 structure is one of sixteen hollow-clay tile round barns believed to have been constructed by Johnston Brothers Clay Works of Fort Dodge, Iowa. Small red tile in the lower level and larger tile above characterized their craftsmanship. The 50-foot wide barn had a centrally located silo, with four horse stalls on one side of the barn interior and cow-milking stanchions on the other half.

The horse-drawn cultivator was patented in 1856.

Black Hawk County

Rownd Barn, 5102 South Main Street, Cedar Falls

Built in 1911 by a Cedar Falls farmer, C. A. Rownd, this round barn is listed on the National Register of Historic Places. Believing that round barns would be more durable in windstorms and more efficient for farming operations, Mr. Rownd had sand and gravel transported to the farm and mixed with cement to form the unique concrete blocks of which the building is constructed. Its unique features are the multiple windows near the eaves and ground floors, allowing for an abundance of natural light. This picture was taken in 1981 before the structure was restored in 1992.

April 3, 1860, the first pony express riders start their routes. October 1, 1896, was the first day of free rural mail delivery. The Pony Express horses had great endurance to travel the nation because they were fed grain from Iowa farms.

— Black Hawk County —

Rownd Barn, after restoration 1992

Measuring 66 feet in diameter, the vertical walls stand 18 feet high. The individual blocks measure 8 inches by 10 inches by 24 inches. This structure stands approximately 46 feet tall.

This photo was taken after the 1992 restoration of the barn shown on the previous page. It is located on the South Campus of Western Home Communities which offers assisted living, nursing care, and a retirement community.

The Homestead Act of 1862, granted 160 acres to settlers who had worked the land five years.

— Black Hawk County —

6312 WEST MOUNT VERNON ROAD, CEDAR FALLS

Though traditional in its 60-foot diameter and its outer wall construction, the uniqueness of this barn is found within. The central clay tile silo has, in its upper portion, a clay water tank devised at the Ames Experiment Station. The twenty-nine dairy cow stanchions facing inward toward the silo are enhanced by preservative-treated wood blocks, which cover the concrete floor of this circa 1915 true-round barn.

Abraham Lincoln created the U. S. Department of Agriculture in 1862.

— Black Hawk County —

8717 Lester Road, Dunkerton

The present owner's great-grandfather, Ace Canfield, had this hollow-clay tile barn built north of Dunkerton in 1918. The carpenter was John Renz. Measuring 70 feet in diameter, it also has a cinder block silo in the middle, which was left over after a previous rectangular wooden barn had burned down in 1917. Its most striking features are the white stone lintels over the door and window casements. The barn has a hand-dug 2-feet-wide by 6-feet-deep concrete foundation and stands approximately 60 to 70 feet tall. The haymow still contains a circular track for a loose hayfork. Roof windows admit light into the upper loft area.

The cost of a rectangular building is thirty-four to fifty-eight percent more than a circular structure.

Bremer County

1123 Easton Avenue, Plainfield

The owners report that this barn is over 100 years old. Used as a granary, it has three interior bin sections. In 2003, a new roof and siding were added, in keeping with the original appearance. There is another larger round barn located on Easton Avenue a few miles away near Nashua.

Sears round barn kit number L2071 in an early 1918 catalog.

No use for a saw on this barn material. The lumber for this Sears barn kit comes already cut and fitted including the siding and roof boards. The barn doors were pre-made and ready to hang in place. A later 1918 ad shows a price increase of approximately $300. As market demand increased, so did the price.

— Bremer County —

Photo by Mike and Ellen Rogers, present owners

1350 260TH STREET, WAVERLY

Built around 1916 by the Johnston Brothers Clay Works, two sizes of tile were used, smaller tile in the lower story and larger tile above. The interior contains large ceiling beams that radiate out from the central silo. Stanchions were used to milk and feed cattle. The house was constructed in 1919 from the same brown, clay tile as the round barn.

The mailbox was also made to resemble a small, red, round barn, but has since been replaced.

Buchanan County

1244 Henley Avenue, Hazleton

Believed to be constructed by Johnston Brothers, this barn is the only working one found that remains operating as built. The Mennonite owners keep the barn well maintained for its dairy enterprise. The interior centrally-located clay silo supports cow stanchions in front of the feed alley. The pump house or milk house in front of the barn has been rebuilt.

Between the eastern and western borders of Iowa, small towns came to life as the prairie soil was turned into farmland. Iowa was divided into 99 counties. All farmers, regardless of residency, could make it to the county courthouse and back home in a day's time.

— Buchanan County —

2325 Benson Shady Grove Avenue, Jesup

An Amish family gave this barn to its current owners. The Amish used it to raise baby chicks. The new owners remodeled it, making the windows shorter They used it to raise chickens and rabbits. Later it was used as a playhouse for young children.

Buena Vista County

261 570th Street, Alta

Outer doors located on the north, south, and east sides of this 40-foot building facilitated easy storage for a large volume of small horse-drawn equipment. With the advent of new larger equipment, the barn's suitability has declined. Framed in plank lumber, horizontal drop siding covers the exterior walls with a cone-shaped, self-supporting, wood-framed, and asphalt-shingled roof.

— Buena Vista County —

![Round barn]

Photo by Marcia and Clyde Krause

6585 90th Avenue, Storm Lake

This place is unique. As you turn in the drive lane, you see three round structures: the water supply tank shown below, the silo in the background, and the barn pictured above. The owner's grandfather, William Mauser, built the round barn in 1910.

The structure is 60 feet in diameter and is built of clay tile. The clay tile walls support the entire barn roof with no interior support. In the original design, the barn was used for milking cows, housing horses, hogs, and feeder cattle. A water tank is near the center. There is a three-thousand bushel oats bin on the upper floor. Hay and straw are distributed by a round track suspended from the roof.

Games, such as horseshoes, making and using homemade stilts, hoops, and sticks provided family fun on the farm in the mid-1800s.

Calhoun County

Charles Knapp Round Barn, Twin Lakes Christian Center, 7718 Twin Lakes Road, Manson

This unique structure is one of only four barns in Iowa known to have a domed roof. The barn measures 60 feet in diameter. It was originally built in 1920 for dairy cattle and breeding Percheron horses. Vertical board-and-batten siding were used on the exterior. There was an interior silo centrally located. Originally constructed with wooden shingles, it was later overlaid with asphalt shingles before being restored again in the mid-1990s. This farm had a round corncrib with a similar dome that was later dismantled.

Milton Hein's extended family donated the barn to the Twin Lakes Christian Center in 1994. The photos pictured on this page were taken in 1995 before the restoration process and move began.

Photo courtesy of Twin Lakes Christian Center

Silos were introduced in the 1870s.

— Calhoun County —

Here comes the tricky part, rounding the corner.

In 1998, the cupola was replaced. Two matching grants in 1999, along with donations, were used to replace both the roof and the haymow floor. In July 2003, this nationally registered Charles Knapp round barn was moved 1-1/2 miles southeast to the grounds of the Twin Lakes Christian Center. The cost was approximately $5 per foot to move the barn.

Curious crowds look on as the domed barn, supported by beams, is moved on a truck.

— Calhoun County —

After many years of planning, fundraising, and volunteer work, this historic round barn was moved successfully to its new location in Manson, Iowa.

The Twin Lakes Christian Center has saved a historic and architectural landmark, one of only four domed round barns in Iowa. The barn is currently used for outdoor education emphasizing creative stewardship of resources, indoor recreation space, community events, concerts, celebrations, exhibits, banquets, and even a few weddings.

Photos this page courtesy of Twin Lakes Christian Center

The restored Charles Knapp Round Barn at the Twin Lakes Christian Center

Carroll County

32805 Hawthorne Avenue, Manning

The modified hip-roof form and non-circular interior appear to be a derivative of Lorenzo Coffin's octagon barn (1867), which was featured in the *Iowa Homestead* magazine. The barn measures 66 feet in diameter. A cupola displays the year 1883. A rectangular interior space with a centrally located driveway allows for a cattle enclosure at the sub-terrain level. At the ground level, hay and machinery storage occupy one side, while granaries and horse stalls are located on the other.

Barbed wire was introduced in 1874.

Cedar County

CEDAR COUNTY FAIRGROUNDS, TIPTON

Octagonal barns were a popular design in the late 1800s.

Cerro Gordo County

Photo by John and Nancy Lass

DOUGLAS-DICKINSON ROUND BARN (BEFORE RESTORATION), 14344 330TH STREET, MASON CITY

This true-round barn with light-brown clay tile was constructed in 1912 with a two-pitched gambrel roof. In the remodeling photos on the next page, the side shed has been removed.

— Cerro Gordo County —

Lower level bricks being replaced

Partially stripped of shingles

All of the shingles removed

Installing the new shingles

Photos by John and Nancy Lass

The Douglas-Dickinson barn was used for raising calves and milking thirty cows until the mid-1960s, when a newer milk parlor was built. After this change, it wasn't as easy to put silage into the silo, but it was convenient to feed the cattle and it kept the silage from freezing. The main big door for loading and unloading of hay faces the west side.

The Douglas-Dickinson Round Barn Fully Restored

Chickasaw County

Darrow Round Barn,
1337 Cheyenne Avenue, Charles City

The large, dark, diamond-patterned tile worked into the barns lighter-colored tile above the main door distinguishes this barn. It was built in 1916 for the Darrow family. Other farmers told the current owners that in hard times, Mr. Darrow went broke, but later was able to buy the farm back.

The self-supporting roof is double-pitched with wooden shingles and small windows that light its loft.

The barn measures 180 feet around and 64 feet in diameter. It has a silo in the middle, which made feeding the cows very convenient. A circular interior allows for both cow stanchions on one half and horse stalls facing the central silo on the other side. The owners milked cows in it until 1979. State inspectors told them they had to close off the silo because it was considered an open feed room, so they quit milking. The owners raised hogs in it until 1985. This barn is no longer standing due to wood rot.

The horse-drawn combine was introduced in 1884.

Clayton County

30648 Garber Road, Guttenberg

Built within a hillside, this building's aesthetic qualities are enhanced by its distinctive gambrel roof, which combines round and sectional cone elements. Wood-framed walls sit upon a stone foundation and are covered with vertical board-and-batten siding.

   Carl H. Ball built this barn, and Jim Burr (who had added steel sides and an asphalt-shingled roof) later restored it.

The University of Illinois and Purdue University were instrumental in the promotion of the efficiencies of the round barn in the midwest and eastern states during the late 1800s and early 1900s.

— Clayton County —

31423 KALE AVENUE, GUTTENBERG

The owner's grandfather designed this barn. It is considered a true "round" dome-shaped barn, one of only four in Iowa. It measures 72 feet in diameter and was built in 1915. The roof has laminated rafters giving it a round shape. It used to have a wood stave silo in the middle. Metal siding distinguishes this barn from others. Entry to the loft is by an earthen ramp between concrete retaining walls. The lower level is used for dairy cattle, and includes stanchions, loose housing pens, and a milk room.

Dallas County

1712 N Avenue, Bouton

The Dan and Larry Taylor families plan to apply for a grant from the Iowa Barn Foundation to fix up this barn and use it for farrowing. The barn has six pie-shaped farrowing pens in it. There is room for a wood-burning stove in the center for winter farrowing.

The round farrowing house and adjacent shed are believed to have been built by Harry Fisher in the 1940s. The rounded sides of the buildings are supposed to direct winter snows to blow around the shed instead of into its interior.

To identify a barn as a mail-order building look for numbers or letters on joists, rafters, or other wooden pieces. A company called Aladdin marked its lumber by lengths. Other companies, such as Sears, put a code on the ends of the lumber that corresponded to the building plans.

Check hardware and equipment for markings. You can also search documentation such as blueprints, working plans, and shipping documentation, if available from present or former owners. Compare catalog drawings or illustrations to the existing structure for a match.

Decatur County

GOODMAN DECAGONAL BARN,
HIGHWAY 69 BETWEEN LEON AND VAN WERT, LEON

Aaron Goodman built this ten-sided barn in 1905 to accommodate 12 horses, a corncrib, and haymow. A rope-and-pulley system was used to transport hay into the haymow from a wagon in the central driveway.

The farm was purchased by Paul and Terri Vaughn from Mr. Goodman's son, Lowell, in 1990. At the time, the Goodman family had owned the farm for over 100 years and had a "Century Farm" certificate. Lowell remembered the construction of the barn and house. He was always proud of the fact that his father, Aaron, had designed, engineered, and built the round barn and house. A neighbor liked the barn so much that he built one for himself.

William Louden of Louden Machinery Works in Fairfield, Iowa, offered the first free barn planning service in 1907. Louden Machinery Works was also noted for the invention and sales of litter carriers and haymow tracks. In September 1867, they patented a hay-stacking device and many other inventions that improved the lives of farmers everywhere.

Delaware County

Photo by Deb Schense

3342 120th Avenue, Coggon

The owner's grandfather, Rob Kirkpatrick, built this round barn in 1914. It cost $1995 to build the barn, excluding labor. All costs were recorded in a handwritten ledger.

The 45-foot silo was built first, then the barn. The man who laid the hollow-tile was paid $195, plus room and board at the farm. It took three months to complete the job.

The feed bunk, which encircles the silo, was also made of tile. This enabled the owners to feed silage inside. They filled the haymow with 4,000 bales of hay. The silage would not freeze as long as the livestock was fed the silage faster than the hay. In 2005, the round barn was completely restored (as shown above) by a local contractor.

Dickinson County

Cable Round Barn,
2308 260th Street, Milford

This large, dark-brown, clay tile barn rested on a concrete foundation with a two-pitched gambrel roof. The site for the barn was purchased in 1912 by W. R. Gillette, and the barn was built the following year by E. Y. Cable, who later purchased the land from Mr. Gillette.

The barn served for many years as a dairy barn and housed six horses, ten head of cattle, and calves. In the summer of 1978, it was struck by lightning and damaged beyond repair. It was taken down in the summer of 2005 because of liability concerns.

Blacksmiths created the first plows. The first light plows could not readily cut through the thick heavy Iowa sod. Heavier plows were created and they needed at least five oxen to pull them. The first time through the field, the plow went only two or three inches deep. A second plowing was required. This was very time consuming as the settlers were able to plow only one to two acres per day.

Dubuque County

11390 North Cascade Road, Dubuque

This round barn was built in 1915, and this photograph was taken in 1995. Thought to be one of sixteen round barns built by the Johnston Brothers, it follows their traditional construction style: 60 feet in diameter, with smaller, red, hollow-clay tile in the lower story and the larger tile above. A large gabled granary in the loft projects out from the roof. With an interior feed bunk below, the loft has a grain storage area but is used mostly for hay.

This barn shown above at 11390 North Cascade Road, was restored and converted into a house. Taken in 2001, this photo shows the dramatic transformation of the barn from the first photo shown above.

Emmet County

250TH STREET, ARMSTRONG

In 1911, construction was started for this 65-foot diameter, true-round barn. A low-pitched, gambrel roof and a first floor of cement block distinguish this barn's appearance. Surrounding the centrally located 16-foot silo on the ground floor are cow stalls on one side, horse stalls on the other, and two pens in the rear. There is a circular hay track in the hayloft above. This barn has not been used since the 1960s.

The United States Government measures land in units of townships and sections.
  A township is comprised of 36 sections, each one mile square.
  A section is made up of 640 acres.
  A quarter section is a 1/2 mile square or 160 acres.
  An eighth of a section is 1/2 mile long by 1/4 mile wide or 80 acres.
  A sixteenth of a section is 1/4 mile square or 40 acres.
  Sections are numbered starting in the northeast corner from 1 to 36.
  Sections are divided into quarters.

Fayette County

2689 Bell Road, Arlington

This unique barn is one of only three known to exist in Iowa. Asphalt shingles overlay the old, wooden-shingled roof and horizontal wood siding envelops the exterior. The inside is an open floor plan, with a feed bunk centered around the interior silo. Originally constructed in 1906 with wood, the silo was later replaced with clay tile.

The specifications for Aladdin Readi-cut barns in the early 1900s included "A-Dollar-A-Knot" guarantee. Siding was guaranteed to be clear of knots.

— Fayette County —

County Road W25, Randalia

This round barn was made from a Johnston Brothers patented design in 1912. The smaller, red-clay tile in the lower story and the larger size above were typical of the firm's design. Johnston Brothers frequently built a straight conical roof with a gabled hay dormer. This barn has a 14-foot diameter silo which is still in use. The barn is used for feeder cattle.

The gasoline tractor was introduced in 1910. The rubber tired tractor first appeared in 1930.

— Fayette County —

Fayette County Fairgrounds, 504 South Vine, West Union

This round clay tile barn shown above was built in 1921 at a cost of $5,000. It was designed for the showing and boarding of cattle during the Fayette County Fair. In the off-season, it was rented as a sales barn for the weekly sales operated by the West Union Auction Exchange until 1995. After it closed, it was remodeled and used for displaying rabbits, chickens, and ducks, etc.

The white Floral Hall round barn was constructed on the fairgrounds in 1913 with the popular fish and turtle tank built in the center of the building. It has always been used for the display of flowers, fruits, and vegetables.

— Fayette County —

Grimes Octagon Barn, Echo Valley Road, West Union

The construction of a gabled hay dormer and the use of shiplap siding make this 1880s octagonal barn distinctive. The builder, Joe Butler, set sturdy white pine framed-timbered walls upon a stone foundation. The core space has a central driveway with stalls on both sides along its length. Although the barn once functioned as a simple animal shelter, it now serves as a modern dairy barn with stainless steel equipment, water bowls, and cork brick floors.

In 1921, five beekeepers formed a cooperative, later known as Sue Bee Honey, to market their 3,000 pounds of Sioux City, Iowa, honey.

Soybeans emerged as a new oilseed crop during the 1930s. They were first grown as a commercial crop in the southeastern United States, arriving in Iowa in the 1920s and 1930s.

Floyd County

SPOTTS ROUND BARN, ST. CHARLES TOWNSHIP,
HIGHWAY 14 WEST, CHARLES CITY

This round barn was built in 1914 and is the only round barn in Floyd County. A patent citation for this barn was issued to Johnston Brothers Works of Iowa on November 19, 1912. Even though slightly smaller in its dimensions, this barn contains a style used by Johnston Brothers with smaller red-clay tile below and larger tile above. It is constructed of clay tile and wood. It measures 55 feet in diameter and 50 feet tall at the peak. A 12-foot diameter silo is in the middle of the barn.

Modern Farm Buildings offered in its 1923 catalog standard oxide red barn paint with optional colors such as French gray, yellow, or maroon.

Franklin County

1380 Hardin Road, on Highways 65 and 20, Iowa Falls*

This Shaker style round barn was built around 1917, as noted by a date scratched in the block. It was originally used as a sheep barn, then as a cattle barn. The current owner's parents purchased the farm in 1939 and used the building for both cattle and hogs. It is currently used for storage.

The barn is approximately 400 feet in circumference. The core space is divided into pie-shaped pens allowing for scores of workspace. There is a 20-foot x 60-foot silo in the center. Cables go over the silo to help hold up the roof. The barn owners claim upkeep on this rolled-asphalt roof is costly.

The present owners purchased the barn approximately 30 years ago; currently, their son lives on the farm.

*__Editor's note__ Although most of Iowa Falls is located in Hardin County, this barn is in rural Franklin County.

In the 1960s farm land was $500 an acre and a bushel of corn yielded around $1.

Hamilton County

2657 210TH STREET, BLAIRSBURG

This 1910 50-foot clay tile structure originated as a combination hog and sales barn with livestock farrowing below and a sales ring above. The interior clay tile silo measures 16 feet in diameter.

The upper sales area is well lit by a row of windows located just below the break in the roofs pitch. Entrance is gained through an earth-filled ramp supported by concrete retaining walls.

In 1997, there were only a little over two million farms left, a number close to that of the 1860s. In 1935, there were 6-1/2 million farms in the United States.

Hancock County

Oudekerk Round Barn,
3055 Maple Avenue, Forest City

Another Johnston Brothers Clay Works structure, this barn adheres to their typical design style, with smaller red-clay tile used below and larger tile used above.

The clay-block walls of this 1915 barn and silo are all that remain to this day. It was in bad shape when purchased by the present owners in 1955.

The top five Iowa agricultural commodities in 2006 were:
1. *Corn valued at $4,206,342,000*
2. *Hogs valued at $4,152,565,000*
3. *Soybeans valued at $2,760,917,000*
4. *Cattle and calves valued at $2,546,466,000*
5. *Dairy products valued at $532,090,000*

Hardin County

Photo by Rod Scott

Slayton Farms Round Barn, 20452 135ᵀᴴ Street, Iowa Falls

Currently owned by the Hardin County Historic Preservation Commission, this clay tile barn was built in 1915 by John T. Slayton. Mr. Slayton commissioned the Johnston Brothers Clay Works of Fort Dodge to construct the round barn. It is the only remaining round barn in Hardin County. The Commission is converting the barn into an agricultural museum.

A center silo measures 67 feet high and the barn is 202 feet in circumference. The two-pitched gambrel roof reaches a height of 18 feet to the first wooden laminate ring and is made of eight one-by-twelve inch beams. The roof was set in place with teams of horses. Each side of the silo has a metal roof aerator. The barn's interior has cattle feeding troughs, draft horse stalls, an oats bin, loft doors, and an air filtration system. Restoration efforts started in 2000 which included a new roof and doors, the result of over $70,000 worth of grants and community support.

Harrison County

Haner Dodecagonal Barn,
2543 130th Street, Moorhead

William B. Haner constructed this barn in 1912 using unusual two-foot-long cement blocks. The upper structure is a 54-foot diameter barn of twelve sides, 14 feet per side, and was constructed in part by lumber salvaged from the nearby old Olympus Church.

William is the current barn owner's great-grandfather. Mr. Haner sold it in his later years, but it was purchased back by William's son, Lester, in 1950.

Although the barn survived hard economic times such as severe drought, depression, and world wars, a raging fire from a lightning strike during a stormy night in July 2002, completely destroyed it. The barn had been re-roofed around the year 2000 and was well on its way to restoration before the fire.

Henry County

Holtkamp Round Barn, 1725 335th Street, Salem

B. J. and Cecilia Holtkamp, shown at left, are the original owners and builders of this 1917 barn. This 50-foot diameter tile barn was designed for horses and other livestock on the ground floor. The main floor housed wagons, corn planters, cultivators, oat seeders, and corn shellers. Animal feed was stored on this level and distributed by chutes with wooden pullout sliding stops at ground level.

The haymow has a circular track that was used to lift loose hay with a huge hayfork from a wagon. The haymow had a central hay chute to the ground floor. The building was designed to handle the loading and unloading of supply wagons into the main floor by using a ramp. Horse-tether rings are visible on the outside walls. In 2000, a new roof was installed.

Howard County

Horky Decahexagonal Barn,
22664 200th Street, Cresco

Since being built in 1920, this rather spacious 70-foot diameter barn has been readapted for its function many times over.

This 16-sided barn sits on a stone foundation and houses a 13-foot centrally located silo. Pie-shaped stalls face inward toward the silo on the lower level while the loft area remains open.

The top five Iowa agricultural exports for 2006 were listed as:
1. *Feed grains and products*
2. *Soybeans and products*
3. *Live animals and meat*
4. *Feed and fodders*
5. *Hides and skins*

Ida County

Waveland Farms, Inc.,
1445 Timber Avenue, Cushing

The year 1914 is displayed on the front, but it was a mistake by the painters. The barn was purchased in 1911. Lumber for this barn was hand-sawn and originally came from the 1904 World's Fair in St. Louis, Missouri. The center part of the barn, three stories in height, was constructed to hold approximately 45 tons of hay.

A gabled roof hay dormer projects from the round structure to match the exterior walls of a wing shed.

Current owners are Albert Henrichsen and sons: Thomas, Vincent, Reed, and Van.

Some of the first designs of the round barn were designed to house cattle on the lower level and hay on the upper level. Newer versions placed the hay in the middle of the barn with the cattle on the interior perimeter. It was believed that a round barn would save farmers time in feeding their livestock.

Iowa County

PLAGGMAN ROUND BARN,
1941 MM AVENUE, MARENGO

This 1912 true-round barn is modeled after a Matt King/Iowa Experimental Station style and is an example of pioneering developments in agricultural buildings and the use of clay tile. It is a bank barn with a lower level designed for cattle. The main level has 30 horse stalls, and a huge 110,000 cubic foot loft capable of holding 200 tons of hay. The building is 85 feet and four inches in diameter, significantly larger than the more traditional Iowa King barns averaging 60 feet. It is considered the largest round barn in Iowa. The interior features a 20-foot diameter clay tile silo standing 45 feet tall. At one time, this barn was home to 30 horses, including large Belgium draft horses.

A neighboring silo once fell on the barn and broken tiles had to be replaced with another color of cinder block. Time took its toll on the roof and in 2003 it was replaced. Repairs were also made to the outer wall. The owner hopes to turn the barn into a center for Iowa farm products. The barn was listed on the National Register of Historic Places in 1986. This barn is rare in its size, craftsmanship, and structural configuration.

Jackson County

Photo by Deb Schense

Dyas Hexagonal Barn,
41279 243rd Street, Bellevue

This unique red eight-sided barn has a round silo in its center. There are only four single-story flat barns in Iowa, and this is the only hexagonal barn among them. Built in 1921, the beams are hand-hewn, and the center silo is made of cedar wood. Stalls are pie-shaped in the interior. The barn is currently used for horses. It is known as the Dyas Hexagonal Barn, named after the family that originally built it.

When restoring historic barns, try to preserve the natural setting such as the nearby woods, ponds, silo, fences, hedges, etc. Paint historic siding instead of using vinyl siding. Try to repair historic windows to keep the original appearance. Retain as many of the original features as possible. Think about using reclaimed wood for repairs.

Jasper County

812 S Commerce Street, Monroe

The house on the premises was built in 1910 and it is likely that the barn was also built around that same time. Made of cement blocks, the barn is very strong and in good condition. At one time, the round barn had been used as a dairy barn.

In the mid-1960s, First Baptist Church purchased the twelve acres where the round barn and house reside for expansion purposes. In 1967, the congregation began to construct a new church. The house is currently used as a parsonage and the barn for storage.

In the 1970s and 1980s, the church youth group played basketball in the hay loft of the barn. Folks at the church still reminisce about playing basketball in the loft when they were kids.

Iowa ranked second in agricultural exports in 2005 with a value of approximately over $4 billion.

— Jasper County —

Halin Octagon Barn, Monroe

No history available.

Johnson County

Miller Round Barn,
3122 500th Street, Riverside

Constructed in 1919, this barn follows the gentle slope of the land where it is built. The ground level loft space is used for hay and grain storage while the lower level houses cow stanchions facing toward a centrally located clay tile silo.

— Johnson County —

Photo by Deb Schense

Roberts Octagonal Barn,
4716 Kansas Avenue SW, Iowa City

This octagon barn was built in 1883. Original barn owner John Roberts, may have borrowed from Lorenzo Coffin's Webster County octagon barn when developing planning concepts. Both barns share the unusually modified hip-roof form and the non-circular interior arrangement making way for multiple functions. This 8-sided barn stands on a foundation of limestone cut 14 to 16 inches in width. Each one of the sides is 26 feet long and the diameter of the barn is 61 feet. The land for the farm was purchased shortly after the Civil War in 1866. Lean-tos were original to the barn and used for added storage and shelter for livestock. Rustic hand-hewn beams frame the interior of the barn.

Iowa was the leading national producer of pork, corn, soybeans, and eggs in the year 2006.

— Johnson County —

Schwab Double-Round Barn,
2501 Sugar Bottom Road NE, Solon

Dick Schwab has built five round barns; this is the first of this type of construction since the 1920s. This unusual structure was built in 1989, shortly before his retirement.

Schwab says he's met his life goals of being debt free by age 40 and retiring at age 48. With 50,000 board feet of lumber needing storage, he redirected his efforts to woodworking, barn building, and volunteering. He remains involved in many non-profit community improvement organizations.

Created from reclaimed lumber, shingles, cement, and straightened nails, this barn provides space for wood storage and equipment. Schwab's father and a college student assisted in the building of this eighteen-sided barn. Schwab commented, "Anyone can build a square or rectangular-shaped barn."

The construction of multi-sided barns was easier than a true-round barn because the builder didn't have to deal with curved boards coming loose. Round barns are being used for farmer's markets, wedding receptions, barn dances, concert halls, bed-and-breakfast attractions, gift shops, antique shops, and fairground exhibits, to name just a few. Check the Internet for round barn events in your area.

— Johnson County —

The Celebration Barn Under Construction
SCHWAB TRUE-ROUND BARN

This 100-foot diameter 24-sided round barn (started in 2005) burned following a lightning strike in 2007. It is being rebuilt with a completion date planned for 2009. The barn will have a big cupola with a widow walk, a main deck, lofts over rooms, men and women's restrooms, kitchen, covered porch overlooking amphitheater and arch, cedar shingles, and a bell-shaped roof with a height of 50 feet. Three French doors will open to the porch overlooking the pond. Schwab has built several ponds on his 92 acres.

— Johnson County —

Photo by Joan Liffring-Zug Bourret

SCHWAB TRUE-ROUND BARN,
2501 SUGAR BOTTOM ROAD NE, SOLON

Started in July 1991, with 100 loads of dirt, Dick Schwab sculpted this structure into the hillside to create an unobtrusive appearance. In the spring, he obtained 30 tons of Stone City stone to cover the wooden interior frame created from recycled old barns or dead trees.

Measuring 40 feet in diameter, this unusual building has six Gothic church windows from Essig, Minnesota. A square dance floor is in the loft, which was used to host a dance at the completion of the barn in August of 1992. There is passive geothermal heating and a wood stove to burn Schwab's "mistakes."

Dick uses the round barn for storage and as a wood shop. As he collects, Schwab says, "my solution is to build more barns." Schwab's rule of stuff is that he always needs ten percent more space for storage.

— Johnson County —

Schwab Hexagonal Round Barn

Dick Schwab rents the sixteen-sided barn (above in the background) for weddings, parties, and community events. It was finished in 2002. Made of Stone City stone with a cedar-shingled roof, the barn is 72 feet in diameter and 40 feet tall. The party barn has three levels, the main floor, loft, and cupola.

Reaching 35 feet in height, the twelve-sided barn (above in the foreground) measures 54 feet in diameter. Constructed in 1997, it also contains three levels and has wood storage and equipment.

Dick built the eight-sided outhouse in 2003, which measures thirteen feet in diameter and is twelve feet tall. It comes complete with two cedar-lined bathrooms that use collected rainwater for a water source.

The stone outhouse between the Schwab barns

Photo by Joan Liffring-Zug Bourret

73

— Johnson County —

The Secrest Octagonal Barn (before restoration), 5750 Osage Street SE, West Liberty

Nineteen-year-old Joshua Secrest moved from Ohio to Iowa in 1869. In 1873, he married a Quaker, Esther Hollingsworth. In 1875, Joshua purchased the farmstead, as his personal contribution to the western expansion of the United States.

Mr. Secrest rode the train from Downey, Iowa, to Colorado and New Mexico to buy calves and sheep and then transport them back home. He and his hired hands herded the livestock through town back to the farm. In the spring, he shipped his fattened livestock to the Chicago markets.

The Secrest farm grew to 520 acres. The average-sized farm in Iowa at that time was 133 acres. In 1883, Joshua and Esther hired the local barn builder, Frank Longerbeam, to plan and construct a large round barn to store hay and house their farm equipment, horses, and milk cows. Mr. Longerbeam constructed a one-of-a-kind barn. It is one of the largest, oldest, and most brilliantly built round barns in the United States. Longerbeam had no formal training in architecture or carpentry, but may have apprenticed with his grandfather.

The use of lamination and the Gothic arched roof are ingenious. It is likely Mr. Longerbeam traveled to Muscatine, Iowa, to buy his lumber from the Hershey Lumber Company. Hershey had a rectangular dairy barn built in the late 1870s that was probably the first use of lamination in a barn. Longerbeam may have seen the Hershey barn and adapted the technique

— Johnson County —

to his round barn. Constructing an arch on the ground and raising it with pulleys and braces was possibly how the Secrest barn was built. The other six additional arched ribs, also composed of eighteen laminated one-by-six inch boards, were then raised one at a time to support the roof.

The Secrest barn is known for its structural sophistication and innovation. The completed barn is an architectural wonder, a monument to the brilliance and determination of our early settlers. The barn once held 300 tons of loose hay in the upper level, breakfast for the 32 horses and 16 cows waiting on the lower level. The neighboring youth, perhaps including ten-year-old Herbert Hoover living in West Branch, must have traveled to marvel at the unique structure. The lofty miniature octagonal cupola is 75 feet above the ground.

Photo by Deb Schense

The Secrest Octagonal Barn (after restoration)

The side shed has two levels. The ground floor was used to feed animals brought in from the field. The upper level of the shed provides support for the unique overhead "railway" car, which runs on a wooden track. The railway car was used to transport feed from the silo or barn to the livestock.

Times were hard for Midwest farmers in the early 1920s and 1930s. The nearby Downey Savings Bank was closed in 1932. The mortgage on the Secrest farm was $20,000 in 1918 and $42,000 in 1920. In 1921, the debt rose to $120,000. This was substantially reduced to $60,000 by 1931. The State of Iowa foreclosed on the property in 1934 with an outstanding debt of $25,000.

In 1974, the barn was added to the National Register of Historic Places.

— Johnson County —

Photo by Joan Liffring-Zug Bourret

Editor Deb Schense in front of the Secrest Barn, holding her historical barn book, Eastern Iowa's Historic Barns and Other Farm Structures: Including the Amana Colonies.

More than 170 million bushels of Iowa corn are processed annually into ethanol. Ethanol from Iowa and U. S. corn growers, reduces our demand for imported gasoline by nearly 100,000 barrels a day.

Keokuk County

Heaton Round Barn, 150th Street, Webster

This round barn was built in 1920. The upper half of the barn is made of 728 curved cement blocks. They measure 9 inches by 21 inches. There are thirteen rows upward by 56 rows around. The top blocks are textured while the lower half is made of curved smooth blocks. There are approximately 300 blocks in the lower half, which is made up of eight rows.

The upper level had a wooden floor. There were four windows and one doorway in the bottom level of the barn. The barn has a dirt floor and a dirt-banked approach to the upper level. A small Ferguson tractor and other equipment were stored inside. Chickens were housed in the lower level.

The structure is currently owned by Roscoe E. Lee of Webster, Iowa.

Ethanol can be made from sugars found in corn, sorghum, wheat, potato skins, rice, or yard clippings. It is made from crops that absorb carbon dioxide and give off oxygen thus reducing greenhouse gases. One bushel of corn can produce 2.7 gallons of ethanol.

Kossuth County

Photo by Evert Broesder

Bates Round Barn,
2608 140ᵀᴴ Avenue, Algona

H. A. Bates, the barn owner's grandfather, built this 45-foot tall barn in 1911 using native trees. It measures 48 feet in diameter. Designed by Horace Duncan of Knightstown, Indiana, a license and permit for $5 were obtained to build the barn in February 1901.

Courtesy of Evert Broesder

— Kossuth County —

Courtesy of Evert Broesder

Photo by Evert Broesder

BATES ROUND BARN

This barn housed three teams of horses and ten dairy cows. Sheep were kept in the back of the barn. Built for horses, this building was designed so a horse and buggy could be driven in, unharnessed, and stabled inside. Six or seven one-by-four inch boards were bent on edge to form the sills. The wooden cedar shingles had to be trimmed to fit as the roof tapered in.

— Kossuth County —

Hendecagonal Barn,
3303 240th Avenue, Titonka

The date 1910 is printed on a brace in this eleven-sided barn. This is probably when the 46-foot diameter barn was built by builder Ben Longbottom. The unusual cone-shaped cupola, perched on an eleven-sided structure, makes this barn unique. The interior houses a 14-foot diameter silo.

The Mayland family purchased this acreage in 1979 from Bonita and Irwin Schmidt. Many people in the neighborhood have helped fill the silo with silage and the haymow with hay. The Schmidts had many different animals when they lived there.

RAGBRAI bicycle riders enjoyed stopping at the barn in 2001. The owners gave a tour of the barn, sold cookies, fruit, and drinks. The owners found it very interesting to visit with people from all over the country.

This barn is featured on the cover. Unfortunately, it was destroyed by fire, and burned down May 29, 2003.

Some derivatives of soybeans are: margarine, salad dressing, mayonnaise, vegetable oil, soy coffee, tofu, and biodiesel fuel.

Lee County

Houston Octagon Barn,
1561 320th Avenue, Fort Madison

Unusual framing and roofing combinations distinctly mark this 1912 octagon barn. Dimension plank lumber is used in the walls and roof rafters of this 60-foot diameter barn. Interior frames of heavy timbered posts and beams secured with wooden pegs support the eight-sections of gambrel roof covered with asphalt shingles. The interior was designed to allow farm equipment to drive through the center.

A new horse barn kit for a 36 x 60' structure, costs approximately $78,000 in 2008. The kit design has eight stalls plus a wash and tack room and a full hayloft. A complete kit price includes all main components such as heavy-duty galvanized stall fronts, chew protection, solid rubber stall mats, and Dutch door turnouts. Concrete, nails, roofing, and labor are not included. Some assembly is required.

Linn County

BRICK CORNCRIB BARN AND SILOS,
3933 NORTH MARION ROAD, ALBURNETT

The original owner, Weaver Witmer, farmed 7,000 acres in Linn and Benton counties. A foreman for Mr. Witmer, Harry Simonsen, constructed these buildings in the mid to late 1930s. He also built several cribs, barns, and other sheds.

Located on the right are two silos with a water storage tank on top to gravity feed the livestock. The center part of the building was used to grind feed. The main crib was used for ear corn storage on each side of the main doorway. Over the doorway were bins for small grain storage.

Lyon County

LYON COUNTY FAIRGROUNDS,
SOUTH 5TH AVE AND TAMA STREET, ROCK RAPIDS

Initial construction of the buildings at the Lyon County Fairgrounds began around 1904. Many who helped with the construction were given shares in the Fair Association. Cement blocks used for the round barn and a few other fairground structures were manufactured and donated by a local plant owned by two men, Latechka and Pettengill.

  Mr. Pettengill wrote in his diary that construction began around the time of the San Francisco earthquake and fire. A half-mile racetrack was built along with a grandstand, some barns, and a floral hall. They rushed the construction so they could have a fair in the new buildings in the fall of 1904. Volunteer efforts have made the fair an annual event since 1893.

Alfalfa (hay) weighs 60 pounds per bushel compressed. A bushel is a metal basket with handles about the size of a modern day round clothes basket. Bushels are used to carry livestock feed and grain.

Madison County

Chautaqua Pavilion Dodecagonal Barn, 1130 West Summit Street, Winterset

Located two blocks north and two blocks east of the Winterset town square, this twelve-sided barn has filled many roles in its lifetime. It began in the early 1880s as a turntable for steam engines on the rail line. It was used this way for a short time because the line changed hands. The railroad used it for storage for several years before selling it. The Chautaqua Association bought it in 1919 and used it for various shows and political events for 23 years. In 1942, the Methodist church bought it and used it seven years for various church and community events. A construction company bought it in 1949 and moved it to its current location. Until then, the building had canvas walls. In 1953, cement walls were cast and raised. Shortly after that, the company went bankrupt. A local businessman/farmer purchased the building and used it for various livestock, but mostly Shetland ponies.

Next, Richard and Linda Wise purchased the property in 1993 and spent many months cleaning it up. They also replaced window panes, removed decades of bird droppings and cobwebs from the rafters, and tons of manure from the floor.

Steel rafters, side supports, and wood in the top of the barn are all original. The barn is currently used for storage and is rented for camper and boat storage

— Madison County —

in the winter. During October, the owners hold an annual flea market. There have been two wedding receptions and various reunion events in the barn over the last ten years.

Mahaska County

LOCKRIDGE ROUND BARN,

2902 JOSEPH LANE, OSKALOOSA

Constructed of cement blocks, this structure has main entry doors from the north, south, east, and west. Assembled in 1927, it was topped with a wood-shingled, two-pitched gambrel self-supporting roof. Lockridge borrowed $2,000 to build the barn and used his 80-acre farm as collateral. Unable to pay off debt ten years later, the farm was sold at a sheriff's foreclosure sale to Harold and Thelma Davis for approximately $2,000. They have owned it for over 70 years.

The haymow can be reached via a ladder through an opening in the center of the barn. The wooden shingles have been replaced once with asphalt shingles, which cost over $20,000.

— Mahaska County —

Southern Iowa Fairgrounds,
615 North "I" Street, Oskaloosa

The Stock Judging Pavilion at the Southern Iowa Fairgrounds was erected at a cost of $15,000 in 1919. The main building measures 156 feet long by 116 feet to the flagpole deck. Concrete, brick, steel, and a small amount of wood were used in the construction. There is enough seating around the show ring to hold over 2,000 people.

The 1921 Sears, Roebuck and Company's book of barns catalog, offered eight good reasons why you should buy Sears' "already cut" Modern Farm Buildings.

1. Our farm buildings are constructed scientifically.
2. Our farm buildings are designed according to the latest sanitation requirements.
3. The framing material is already cut and fitted, reducing waste and labor.
4. Any handy man can build our "already cut" buildings.
5. You will not be required to purchase any extra materials.
6. We guarantee our materials are of good grade.
7. Our buildings have proved correct and practical in all details.
8. You can buy any building in our catalog of $500 or more on easy payments.

Marion County

Photo by d'Lyse Abukaf

James Round Barn,
708 Rutledge Street, Knoxville

Built in 1911, an owner expanded this round barn by surrounding four-fifths of it with a one-story addition. The remaining section is coupled with a one-and-one-half story wing shed. It has a two-pitched gambrel roof with wooden shingles.

The outside is covered with horizontal shiplap siding. The barn measures 76 feet in diameter and the interior silo is fourteen feet in diameter. The interior is laid out in the same circular construction with feed bunks attached to corn and grain cribs aligning the outer walls.

At 15.5 percent moisture, shelled corn weighs 56 pounds per bushel and corn on the ear weighs 70 pounds per bushel. Oats weigh 32 pounds per bushel.

Marshall County

1708 Reed Avenue, Marshalltown

Current barn owners believe William and Carrie Paisley built this barn between 1899 and 1904. The building was used solely for hog farrowing for the Paisley's purebred Hereford hogs.

The center area of the barn serves as the feeding and watering area for all the pie-shaped pens that are formed by the shape of the building. This prevented having to enter any of the stalls and allowed the cleaning to be done with a minimum of lifting or carrying. Both feed and water were stored in the silo at the center with the water tank above the grain. The floor of the grain storage compartment is cone shaped so grain would flow out when the chute was opened to the feeding and watering area.

A storage space encircles the entire circumference of the building. There is a hayloft approximately eight feet above the ground floor. There is a fold-up ladder to climb up to the loft. On the underside of the loft is a metal track that supports a litter carrier for removal of manure. The carrier is suspended about four feet above the floor of the building. It could slide around the entire building and then out the north door where the track extended outside for dumping the waste.

There was also a furnace to heat the building. To have an enclosed building with heat, feed, and water seems pretty innovative for turn of the century technology. The owners would like to restore the century-old barn, but, even with the possibility of matching grants, the cost is prohibitive.

— Marshall County —

Decahexagonal Barn,
2851 Jessup Avenue, Melbourne

Almost round, this smaller barn was built with 16 sides.

In 2008, the cost to reshingle a barn roof with asphalt shingles can cost upwards from $20,000 to $30,000 or more depending on the barn size.

— Marshall County —

Dobbin Round Barn,
2551 Brown Avenue, State Center

"Barrel Barn No. 214" built in 1919, was the handiwork of the Gordon-Van Tine Company, a Davenport, Iowa, manufacturer of pre-cut mail-order barns. Barn owner Henry Dobbin, saw the same barn three miles down the road on the Yordy farm and decided he wanted one just like it.

Measuring 60-feet in diameter, this barn has a circular interior design with half of it for horse stalls and the other half for cows. The self-supporting gambrel roof is covered with asphalt shingles. The cupola is made with louvered ventilated windows.

Annually, a hen lays on average 268 eggs. Have fun egg hunting.

History of the Round Barn Mail-order Kits

The late 1800s saw a dramatic increase in immigrants entering the United States. Many of the newcomers were interested in buying land and building barns. The popularity of mail-order catalogs, farm journals, and building design books, along with the availability of pre-cut-lumber and railroad transportation, helped spark an interest in mail-order barn kits. New legislation helped to promote barn safety and health for the farmer and his livestock, making barn kits even more appealing.

Beginning in 1910, the Gordon-Van Tine Company located in Davenport, Iowa, boasted of being the first business to offer pre-cut, pre-fabricated houses. The firm also offered pre-fabricated mail-order barns under their own name, and for Sears, Roebuck and Company. The craftsmanship of the carpenter was excellent, and the scrap materials were almost non-existent, lowering the cost of pre-fabricated buildings. A mail-order round barn kit for a structure measuring 60 feet in diameter by 48 feet tall was offered in 1918 at $1,627. Sears included standard pre-made doors for the round barn.

World War I slowed the production of the mail-order barns for a time. The Great Depression of the 1930s and the onslaught of World War II also hurt the quality of the mail-order barn business. The lack of quality materials and labor during this time period led to the demise of many mail-order companies.

Sears round barn kit number 2071 in a 1918 catalog.

History of the Round Barn Mail-order Kits

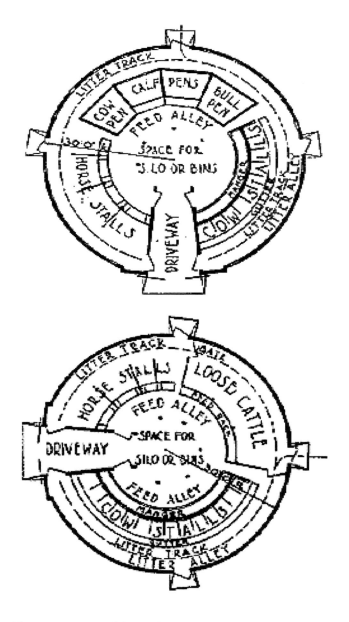

Two possible interior round barn floor configurations are shown from a 1918 Sears catalog. Space for the silo or bins is in the center. The round layout made it easy for a horse-drawn wagon to circle around as opposed to backing up.

History of the Round Barn Mail-order Kits

ALREADY CUT AND FITTED PRICE $1,627.00 AND UP

A Round Barn, 60 Feet in Diameter, "Already Cut" and Fitted

Sears round barn ad in 1918

What do you get for $1,627 in 1918? All framing lumber is number one yellow pine. The outside walls are covered with double V vertical siding of cypress deemed, "The Wood Eternal." The barn doors, produced by hand, were made of cypress also.

For an additional $55 you could upgrade to select cypress siding. The outside walls were advertised by Sears to withstand the weather for a lifetime. The roof was covered with extra thick red-cedar shingles. Hinged windows with an opening of 1-foot 10-1/2 inches by 2 feet 9-1/2 inches were furnished with the barn kit.

Hardware, such as latches, bolts, screws, and nails, etc., was included in the price, as well as two coats of oxide red paint for the exterior and white paint for the trim. Other paint options were available from this catalog.

Ventilating systems, cupolas, barn equipment, silos, and foundation material were not included in the price. The barn was to be built on a two-foot concrete foundation.

All pieces were pre-cut and the doors were pre-assembled. The large driveway doors came with the highest priced hangers, "The Roll Rite Hangers." Free, easy to understand building plans were included. Sears advertised that the easy-to-follow directions displayed where every piece fits. The pre-cut barn kit was advertised to make a good investment and a great saver of time and labor.

Monona County

15755 State Highway 141, Mapleton

The barn's original owner, Seth Smith, was a well-known auctioneer who had this barn built in 1921 to use for selling his purebred cattle. Its open-spaced interior is now used as a general-purpose barn for livestock and mainly as a farrowing house for Duroc hogs. The current owners bought the farm in 1949.

It is estimated that in 2008, wine sales in Iowa will be more than $22 million. Iowa boasts 70 wineries in 2008, with wine sales of 256,000 gallons for the fiscal year ending June, 2007. Visitors to Iowa wineries during 2006 to 2008 totaled more than 400,000.

Montgomery County

2559 140ᵀᴴ Street, Red Oak

Built in 1912, this 60-foot diameter barn contains an 18-foot diameter wood stave silo. Double sliding doors on both the front and rear sides of the barn allow for easy access to the circularly arranged interior, especially for navigating around the central silo.

In Iowa, there were 84,451 men and 6,204 women as principal farm operators according to the 2002 Census of Agriculture. The average age is 54.3.

— Montgomery County —

1680 U. S. Highway 71, Villisca

J. B. Kimmel built this 60-foot diameter hog barn in 1917. It has 24 sides and is nearly round. Hog pens were placed on the outside as well as on the inside of the barn. A team of horses and a manure spreader made efficient work of cleaning this barn by circling the interior. Later, this barn was used for housing cattle.

Iowa's bees produce approximately 2.18 million pounds of honey annually. Iowa's honey is marketed to the Middle East, Far East, Europe, and South and Central America. Honey is one of the purest foods available.

Page County

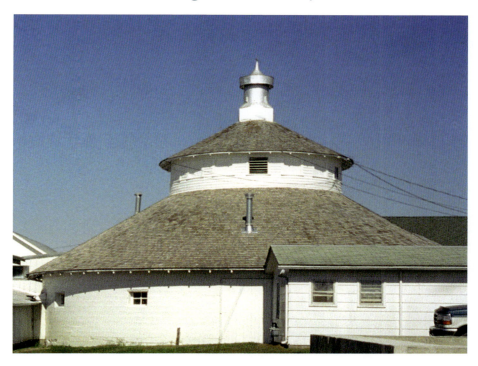

CLARINDA LIVESTOCK AUCTION, NEAR PAGE COUNTY
FAIRGROUNDS, GARFIELD ST., CLARINDA

This barn was built by the city of Clarinda as an auction barn in 1929. It has been owned by the Crawford family since 1946.

H AVENUE, ESSEX

No history available.

97

— Page County —

Braymen Decahexagonal Barn,
Section 15 Morton Township, Shenandoah

This sixteen-sided barn was built in 1914. This 90-foot diameter, single-story barn has a "tent-like" pole support system for its low-pitched roof. Three stalls, a bin, and a loose livestock housing area surround the center, which is filled with hay. Duane Rexroth purchased the barn in 1984. In 2005, a fresh coat of paint was applied.

Both soybeans and wheat weigh 60 pounds per bushel.

Plymouth County

Photo by Rachael Strickel

Mohan Round Barn,
17624 Fir Avenue, Akron

Quadruple roof dormers placed just below the hip of the barn's second pitch differentiate this barn. Its exterior walls are constructed of red-clay tile. The barn has been torn down since this picture was taken.

Shakers, a religious group in the eastern United States, believed that evil spirits wouldn't have a corner to hide in if the Shakers built round barns.

— Plymouth County —

Photo by d'Lyse Abukaf

Tonsfeldt Round Barn,
500 4th Avenue NE, Le Mars

Over a three-year period beginning in 1918, Peter Tonsfeldt built this prominent barn to display his purebred Hereford cattle. By originally building on a sheltered hill slope, he gained basement floor space for a feed bunk and loose stock pens. The main floor houses a feed alley and fourteen cattle stalls, accommodating two head each. Each stall is equipped with a hay manger and two boxes for grain. A manure carrier hangs from a track, circles behind the stalls, and exits out a door to be dumped outside.

At the barn's center stands a forty-foot high by twelve-foot across wooden laminated silo lined with steel mesh and plastered with concrete. The upper floor has room for many tons of hay surrounding the silo. The disproportionately high, 65-foot Gothic arched roof, provides a striking appearance. This building measures 62 feet across.

The Langel brothers of Le Mars donated it to the fair board after they purchased the land where it was located. Berghorst and Sons moved it to the fairgrounds in September of 1981 at a cost of $8,000. The Plymouth County Fair Board also paid another $5,000 for moving wires and other related costs. Two local couples raised $16,000 in donations to help with the moving expenses. It was reshingled at a cost of $16,400 in materials and labor. The rest of it was restored in early 1982 and opened for that year's fair. During the fair, the barn is used to display arts, crafts, and photography on the upper level and horticulture items on the lower level.

Pocahontas County

Photo by Rachael Strickel

Highway 3 West, Pocahontas

Adolph and Margaret Schreyer built this barn. This single-story barn stands on a vacant farmstead. Its walls are constructed of clay tile, and its cone-shaped roof is made of wooden shingles. The facility was used as a livestock barn for mainly hogs, cattle, and horses, as well as storage for hay, straw, and small machinery in the later years. The farm is currently owned by Dean and Norma Jean Seehusen of Pocahontas, Iowa.

A dome-shaped roof, that is self-supporting, can nearly double the capacity of the haymow.

Pottawattamie County

11646 290ᵀᴴ Street, Silver City

No history available.

A milk cow produces approximately 2,410 gallons or 38,560 glasses of milk per year. The major breeds of milk cows in the United States are: Ayrshire, Brown Swiss, Guernsey, Holstein, Jersey, and Milking Shorthorn. The most common dairy breed is the Holstein, with black and white spots. They produce the most milk.

Poweshiek County

THORN BROTHERS OCTAGON BARN,
JACKSON TOWNSHIP, SECTION 4, 2 MILES EAST OF MONTEZUMA
ON HIGHWAY 85, MONTEZUMA

The Thorn Brothers of Montezuma built this barn in 1916. A steeply pitched hay dormer with three equally pitched gabled-roof dormers enhance the cone roof of this notable octagonal barn. The present owner's father, Henry Hutchinson, bought the farm with the barn in 1930. The barn is still in use.

On average, it takes approximately 500 years to create one inch of soil. To prevent soil erosion, some farmers have turned to terrace farming in hilly areas. Terrace farming consists of building a series of steps supported by sod. Each level slows the flow of water runoff, slowing the erosion process. It also allows tillage to areas that formerly could not be farmed.

Ringgold County

Buck Nonagon Barn,
2061 180th Street, Diagonal

This nine-sided barn with a diameter of 65 feet was built in 1909. Though similar in design to a barn built by an Illinois farmer, Lloyd Jones, that was featured in *Wallace's Farmer* magazine in 1903, this barn stands alone within Iowa. The central part of the barn has six sides. A nine-section wing shed is built almost all the way around it. Alternating rectangular and pie-shaped sections comprise the roof.

One bushel of soybeans yields 11 pounds of soy oil and 48 pounds of high protein meal. The national average soybean yield is approximately 40 bushels per acre. An acre of ground is 43,560 square feet.

Scott County

Knoll Crest Farm, Nebergall Round Barn, 9478 145th Street, Davenport

The Nebergall family had this round barn built in 1914 by Benton Steele, a contractor from Halstead, Kansas. The 56-foot diameter design has a two-pitched gambrel wood-shingled conical roof with cupola. A driveway divides the interior circular arrangement. Lower floor walls are made of clay, while the upper level walls are of lumber with board-and-batten siding.

It remained with the Nebergall family until 1992 when the Knoll Crest Farm was sold to John Penne. He re-roofed the barn in 1998 with wooden shingles and kept the hayforks and manure track system in working order. The loft area is used for storage.

In 2006, Iowa produced 510 million bushels of soybeans.

— Scott County —

John from the Benton Steele contractors wrote the Nebergall family on January 7, 1915, after the construction of their barn.
Here is an excerpt of the letter he wrote in his own words:

"I have been thinking for some time that I would write you, but always too busy, it seems.

We built four barns after leaving your place, and wound up a few days before Christmas, all the old crew and two new men remaining together till the finish.

...

I hope you enjoyed the barn and by the way, have you ever had any more pictures made, since it was finished and the pictures we got at your place were so poor, that I don't think the boys ever sent you any, maybe they did, I have not kept track as I should.

How is the building outlook in your neighborhood?

Would you care to give me the name and address of the old gentlemen who liked the barn so well? I think he is a fruit or commission merchant over at Davenport, has a farm up in Wisconsin.

Mrs. Nebergall, I want here to remind you of my sincere gratitude and appreciation, for the courteous treatment and generous hospitality accorded while with you. The boys often said, that we never were more considerately treated in all our rounds. The evening we left is vividly before me as I write.

Hoping you are all real well and to hear from you at your leisure, I remain, John, joining,

Yours Very Cordially,
Benton Steele

A jumbo hopper train car can hold 100 tons or 3,500 bushels of grain. One barge can hold approximately 1,500 tons or 52,500 bushels of grain.

— Scott County —

23980 Great River Road, Le Claire

The former octagon barn pictured above was built in 1907. The barn measures 50 feet across and at one time had a 12-foot diameter silo inside. It was used as a reception hall for many years. In 1989, the barn was framed as livable space. There are eight logs in the basement that are the main support poles for the house. These logs were cut from the trees on the farm's property.

In 2006, Iowa produced 2.05 billion bushels of corn.

Sioux County

SECTION 7, GARFIELD

Bearing a close resemblance to the McLean County, Illinois, barn featured in John Geiger's magazine, this round barn is located in rural Iowa near the border town of Hudson, South Dakota. It has a double metal roof, clay tile first-floor walls, and horizontally applied wood siding on its upper portions. Although the construction date is unknown, the barn was featured in an issue of a 1920s farm magazine.

In 2006, the state of Iowa had 3.95 million head of cattle, 17.2 million head of hogs, 235,000 head of sheep and lambs, 51.6 million egg layers, and 274 million pounds of turkey.

Story County

Photo by Evert Broesder

Belcher Round Barn, 28103 640th Avenue, Nevada

Built in 1916, the original stucco-surfaced roof provided an interesting visual effect, but it has since been converted to shingles. In 1999, lightning struck the dome and the owner has since repaired it. Clay tile walls extend the entire height of the barn.

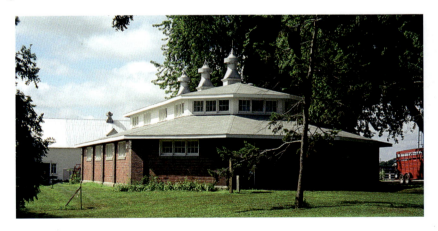

Iowa State University, Hayward and Mortensen Roads, Ames

This oval clay tile dairy barn has seating for both students and spectators on the university campus. The facility is used for teaching livestock selection and management. High windows allow for natural lighting. Built in approximately 1921, it was restored around the year 2000.

Tama County

Hayward Round Barn, 1520 Highway V-37, Dysart

Another round barn with all the earmarks of Johnston Brothers construction, this approximately 1917 structure features a long rectangular clay tile addition. Otis J. Hayward Sr., owned the farm at the time it was built. In 1960 or 1961, a tornado blew off the top of the barn, several feet of the silo, the roof, and most of the large haymow. The roof was repaired soon after. As a result of the damage, the barn now stands a few feet shorter than the original structure. A picture of the damaged barn was featured on the front page of the *Waterloo Courier*.

A new roof was put on in 1965, but the brick work was from the original barn. The owner has been told that the corncrib near the barn is of more historical interest than the barn. Some day the owner would like to renovate the barn.

Today there are approximately one billion acres of farmland nationwide. In 2006, Iowa had 31,500,000 acres in farmland.

— Tama County —

BEHRNS ROUND BARN, 1094 P AVENUE, TRAER

Photo courtesy of owners

Designed by John Ames of Traer, this barn was built in the 1920s. The building is original except for the three large interior sliding doors. The building and interior silo are made of hollow tile, and the floor is cemented. It is topped off with a dome and cupola. The two-pitched gambrel roof is unusual in that its steep lower half is constructed of trapezoidal sections, with a lower pitch extending upward from the hip.

The silo measures 16 feet by 40 feet tall. The barn totals 160 feet in circumference and 22 ½ feet to the eaves with a 50-foot diameter.

When the barn was active, it was used for raising feeder cattle. It is currently used for storage. In 1986, this building was entered in the National Register of Historic Places.

Taylor County

© *Ceiling photo by Carolyn Fox*

Taylor County Museum Grounds, Cameron Round Barn, 1001 Pollock Blvd., Bedford

An early Taylor County resident, J. E. Cameron, constructed one of the earliest first true-round European-type barns in Iowa around 1907. The

— Taylor County —

round shape was designed to withstand high winds and severe storms. Given that this roof has no interior posts to support its middle, the steep pitch must have played a contributing role in the roof's longevity as it relieves weight from its rafters.

The barn was built just south of Lenox and was commonly referred to as the Lenox Round Barn. It stands over 50 feet high and is 64 feet in diameter. The circumference measures 220 feet. Dick and Evelyn Brammer donated the barn so that it could be relocated to the Taylor County Museum grounds for restoration and public exhibition.

The move was broken down into two phases. The first phase involved removing the cupola and complete disassembly of the roof. The roof was separated into two sections with each piece being lifted by crane from the barn. The remainder of the barn was then split into two sections and lifted by crane onto a transport vehicle. All the pieces were then moved down the highway to the Taylor County Museum grounds.

The second phase entailed reassembly of the barn pieces at the new location. Original or similar materials were used in order to preserve the historic integrity of the barn. Many volunteers participated.

To see this magnificent structure, stop by the Taylor County Museum. The barn is open for public exhibition.

CORNER OF HIGHWAYS 2 AND 25, BLOCKTON

The current owners bought the farm in 1960, and the round barn was present at that time. It has angled partitions with a center round area. The owners farrowed baby pigs and baby lambs in the barn. Their daughter has many fond childhood memories of playing with the lambs and bottle-feeding them.

Van Buren County

Silver Round Barn,
17451 260th Street, Cantril

It is the two-pitched gambrel roof with its eight dormers on the lower part and three on the upper that gives this early 1900s barn great distinction. It was constructed at a cost of $20,000 during the years 1917 through 1919. F. F. Silver, proprietor of Wickfield Farms, designed the 52-foot diameter sales barn with seating for up to 700 and with kitchens downstairs to feed the crews.

Upstairs there were rooms for his employees, each with their own dormered window to view the kingdom built on the purebred Hampshire hog market. Mr. Silver had enough farmhands to field a ball team, so many in fact, that it caught the attention of newsreel crews from Hollywood. The publicity certainly helped create high prices in the auction ring. An auction in February of 1920 brought $573 a head for 52 sows, for a total of $29,796.

As the Depression settled across the countryside, Mr. Silver and hundreds of other Van Buren County farmers went bankrupt. The sales barn was then

— Van Buren County —

turned into a roadhouse and the hayloft became a dance floor.

Prohibition opened up new business opportunities for the barn's owners. They were raided for selling liquor a few times, although history buffs gloss over the gambling, cockfights, moonshine, and the ladies of the night who took up residence on the second floor.

Still quite sound, the structure is used primarily for storage.

Photo by Terry Hostetler

CRAMLET ROUND BARN, 11256 CR V64, DOUDS

Louden Machinery Company based in Fairfield, Iowa, was known as a provider of farm building plans and equipment. It is believed that this 1921 round barn is the only one in Iowa to have been designed by them. It was only one of three built in Iowa with a domed roof. The dome collapsed in 1970 and was replaced by an asphalt-shingled cone roof and a metal cupola.

The top Iowa commodity exports in 2006 were tractors at $712 million, corn (except seed corn) at $278 million, and pork meat at $244 million.

— Van Buren County —

Photo by Rachael Strickel

French Round Barn,
32303 277th Street, Farmington

It is believed that Bill French built this barn in 1928. It measures 60 feet in diameter with a 12- by 40-foot central silo.

The original roof was an impressive circular hip roof design with a big haymow door dormer facing south over the south door. The mow track made a complete circle. The hauling rope was pulled by a complicated pulley setup through the east door by a team of horses or a small tractor. The haymow could store a large amount of hay. The owners put loose hay up in this manner until the mid-1960s.

After the late 1960s, the roofing failure caused sheathing and the haymow floor to rot to the point that the owner decided to remove the roof and put up the current eight-segment steel roof. The ground level of the original design, of necessity, had to have two concentric rings of four-inch steel pipes filled with concrete for haymow floor supports. As a result, there was no way to get even a small wagon or manure spreader inside. Everything had to be carried in and out by hand. The owner had plans to use the silo again, but found it to be too labor-intensive and impractical. Despite being an impressive structure to behold, it was a very impractical design in the end.

Warren County

Nutting Octagon, 17544 Highway S23, Milo

David Nutting, great-grandfather of Esther (Nutting) Merrell, came here from Massachusetts in the 1860s in an oxcart. The Nutting family erected this barn by 1900. Very similar in design to the nine-sided barn in Ringgold County, Iowa, the plan approximates that of an Illinois stock barn owned by Lloyd Jones. This farm has been in the family ever since it was built, making it a century farm.

The east side of the barn had horse stalls, and the west side was designed for milk cows. The center part of the barn has a second-story haymow. The tall central section has a rectangular interior arrangement flanked by grain bins and open space. Hay was elevated into the haymow using a rope and hayfork. A hay track was installed from the top plate on the north side to a heavy rafter. Hay could be pitched on the east, south (shed side), and the west.

A driveway is in the center with grain bins on the sides. A wing shed surrounds most of the exterior.

This building was placed on the National Register of Historic Places about 30 years ago.

Washington County

2750 Highway 22, Riverside

No history available.

Water damage is the most common cause for wood decay. Insects prefer to attack damp wood. Keep the barn roof, windows, and cupola in good repair to maintain the structure.

— Washington County —

Johnson Decahexagonal Barn, 1480 Ginkgo Avenue, Wellman

The owner's father, Thomas R. Johnson, built the sixteen-sided round barn in about 1921 two to three miles south of Wellman. The barn was built to house hog farrowing production. Within the last few years, it has been re-sided and re-roofed.

Each of the sixteen sides measures eight feet wide, and the barn measures 40 feet across.

The barn has been used for hogs and cattle in the past, with fifteen pens built around the perimeter of the barn. This building was placed on the National Registry of Historic Places in 1986.

In 2006, Iowa, with an estimated population of 2,982,085 had approximately 5-1/2 hogs per person.

Wayne County

The International Center for Rural Culture and Art, Inc., One mile east of Allerton

Late in the summer of 1991, citizens learned that the last remaining round barn in Wayne County was about to be sold. Afraid that the new owners would demolish the historically significant structure, a core group formed a non-profit corporation to purchase the 93-acre farm. The International Center for Rural Culture and Art, Inc., was formed. The purpose of the organization is to educate the public about past and present rural life through historical preservation.

The 50-foot diameter barn features a support-free loft due to its unique spider web construction. Restoration work includes new doors, windows, siding repair and replacement, a new cedar shake roof, cupola repairs, and a new staircase to the haymow.

The average Iowa farm size according to the 2002 agricultural census was 350 acres.

Winnebago County

19960 500ᵀᴴ Street, Scarville

The hollow-clay tile construction is the handiwork of the Johnston Brothers. The eight-section conical roof possesses a very large hay dormer. Surrounding the interior clay silo are cow stanchions, horse stalls, and calf pens. The barn was no longer used after 1970.

University research shows that a circular structure is much stronger than a rectangular building.

Winneshiek County

KINNY OCTAGON,
3706 HIGHWAY 52 NORTH, BURR OAK

This octagon barn has a similar look to the Lorenzo Coffin barn of Webster County with its modified hip-roof form and rectangular interior arrangement. An article was published about the Lorenzo Coffin barn in 1883, and it is assumed that this barn was built after that year. Each of the octagonal sides measures 20 feet. A central driveway divides eight animal pens, a feed room, and an old milk room. Loose hay was loaded into the loft with the aid of a large wooden pulley.

The average price of Iowa farm land in 2007 sold for $3,908* per acre. In Iowa, the price of a bushel of corn in 2008 is in the $5 range. The cost of a new combine is a staggering $100,000 to $150,000.

* According to the Iowa State University Extension annual survey.

— Winneshiek County —

1912 Glenville Road, Decorah

This may be one of the oldest standing octagonal barns in the state, although its exact year of construction is unknown. The interior diameter measures 68 feet with a 14-foot diameter wood stave silo. The basement level has housed many animals over the years.

Later, metal siding was placed over the horizontal siding. In the 1970s, a storm dismantled a cupola and windmill on the roof. More recently, the roofing material was replaced.

Most of Iowa's farmers raise corn, soybeans, cattle, and hogs, but a few raise other animals such as llamas, goats, emus, turkeys, chickens, sheep, and horses.

— Winneshiek County —

Octagon Barn,
1173 Highway 9 East, Decorah

Initially built in 1950, the silo was used for storing chopped hay. The barn was originally used for beef cattle, but now it is used for storage.

To determine the number of bushels of grain in a bin: multiply the length by the width by the depth in feet. Divide the result by 1.25.

E.g.: 20 feet long x 8 feet wide x 10 feet tall = 1600 / 1.25 = 1280 bushels

About the Photographer

Luella Hazeltine

Luella Hazeltine was born in Cedar Rapids, Iowa, in 1929. She has lived in Linn County all of her life. After high school graduation, she worked for Quaker Oats for forty years, where her husband was also employed. He was also a honey producer for a while. After her retirement, Luella spent the next decade, and more, finding and photographing the barns in this book.

Luella shot the majority of the photographs, but her nieces, Rachael Strickel and d'Lyse Abukaf, also played a hand in taking a few of the photographs. When Luella viewed a public television show about barns, she was inspired to find out more about them in her home state of Iowa. She began gathering the photos in 1993. Penfield Books asked to publish them to preserve in print Iowa's agricultural heritage. The negatives are Luella's gift to the State Historical Society of Iowa.

About the Editor

Deb M. Schense

An Iowan all her life, Deb Schense grew up on a farm (with a late 1800s barn) northeast of Waverly, Iowa. She earned an Associate of Applied Science degree in computer programming from Kirkwood Community College and a Bachelor of Business Administration in Management Information Systems from the University of Iowa.

Since graduating, Deb has worked in corporate America, the federal government, computer consulting, and self-employment.

She is an author of *Eastern Iowa's Historic Barns and Other Farm Structures: Including the Amana Colonies* with two editions: black-and-white, and color. She is working on a comedy screenplay and book entitled *Extended Vacation*. For more information, you may visit her website at: www.thecorridormall.com/deb

Giants of Agriculture

During the past centuries, three men with ties to the State of Iowa have made singular contributions to the world through research, development, teaching, and diplomacy.

Norman Borlaug (1914–)

Borlaug, a descendant of Norwegian immigrants, was born on a farm near Howard/Chickasaw County in northeast Iowa. His earliest academic experience began in a one-room Iowa schoolhouse. Enrolling at the University of Minnesota in 1933, Borlaug obtained his PhD. in plant pathology and genetics in 1942.

Borlaug's career, inventing and developing high-yield, disease-resistant wheat varieties, revolutionized the production of food worldwide. He has been called "the father of the Green Revolution." In Mexico, Pakistan, and India, he nearly doubled wheat yields in those and other countries. Today, Borlaug is one of the very few individuals who has been awarded the Nobel Peace Prize (1970), the Presidential Medal of Freedom (1977), and the Congressional Gold Medal (2007). His Congressional Gold Medal citation reads in part: "Dr. Borlaug has saved more lives than any other person who has ever lived…"

Henry A. Wallace (1888–1965)

Born on a farm in Adair County, Iowa, Wallace graduated from Iowa State College in Ames in 1910. He founded Hi-Bred Corn, a company that later became Pioneer Hi-Bred, a major agricultural corporation. Wallace's birthplace is now called, "The Henry A. Wallace Country Life Center." The farmstead is open to the public at 2773 290th Street, near Orient, Iowa.

In 1933, Wallace became Secretary of Agriculture in Franklin Roosevelt's administration and was the principle architect for the New Deal's farm program. Wallace resigned in 1940 to become FDR's Vice Presidential running mate. He served as Vice President during America's involvement in World War II. He very narrowly escaped becoming President after Roosevelt's death. Wallace lost out to Truman at the 1944 Democratic Convention. Today, the Henry A. Wallace Beltsville Agricultural Research Center in Maryland is named for him. It is the largest agricultural research complex in the world.

George Washington Carver (1860–1943)

One of the earliest advocates of sustainable agriculture, Carver was born into slavery in Newton County, Missouri, and first came to Iowa in 1887. He then enrolled in Simpson College, Indianola, Iowa, as its second African-American student. In 1891, Carver transferred to the Iowa State Agricultural College in Ames, where he was the first black student and later its first black faculty member. Carver remained in Ames until 1896 when he departed to lead the Agricultural Department at Tuskegee Normal and Industrial Institute in Alabama for 47 years, until his death in 1943.

Iowa helped form Carver's important career as one of the nation's foremost botanists, researchers, and educators. He believed in bringing agricultural education directly to farmers, through extension work. Carver's fame was based on his research into alternatives to cotton production, resulting in his advocacy of peanut and sweet potato production and development.

Bakkum Pines

Fred Easker painted this oil painting without a barn where a homestead may have once stood in the midst of trees in between Lansing and Waukon, Iowa in Allamakee County. If we fail to maintain Iowa's barns, this could be our rural landscape of the future. Fred, who has studios in Cedar Rapids and Lansing, documents Iowa landscapes in his work.

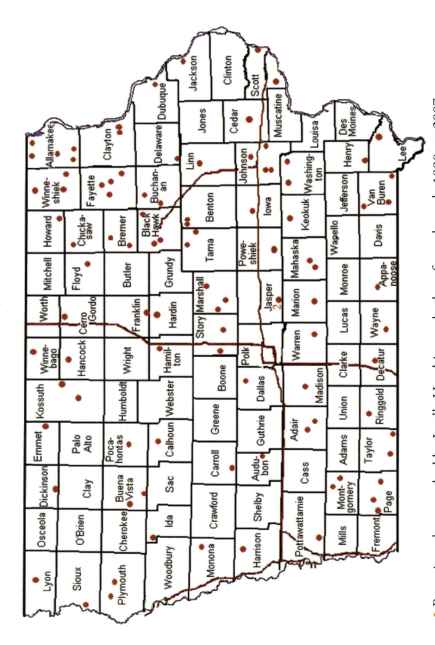

• Barn sites photographed by Luella Hazeltine and others from the early 1990s to 2007.
Many thanks to the Iowa Department of Transportation for granting permission to modify and publish their county map.